This book is a gift of the
Cops 'n' Kids Literacy Program

To: _____

From: _____

Date: _____

Quota International
of Bethlehem

WILLOW LANE ELEMENTARY
INCREDIBLE HAWKS

1762
ALLENTOWN PA
POLICE

Ernest Rutherford

and the Birth of the Atomic Age

Profiles in Science

Ernest Rutherford and the Birth of the Atomic Age

Library of Congress Cataloging-in-Publication Data

Baxter, Roberta, 1952–
  Ernest Rutherford and the birth of the atomic age / by Roberta Baxter.
    p. cm. — (Profiles in science)
  Includes bibliographical references and index.
  ISBN 978-1-59935-171-1 (alk. paper)
1. Rutherford, Ernest, 1871-1937. 2. Physicists—New Zealand—Biography.
3. Nuclear physics—History. I. Title.
  QC16.R8 B38 2011
  530.092--dc22
  [B]

                                    2010049096

e-book isbn: 978-1-59935-275-6

Printed in the United States of America
First Edition

Book cover and interior designed by:
James Slate, JMS Design
Chicago, IL

Ernest Rutherford

and the Birth of the Atomic Age

ROBERTA BAXTER

MORGAN
REYNOLDS
PUBLISHING

Greensboro, North Carolina

Contents

New Zealand Boy

Ernest Rutherford was always proud that he was born and raised in New Zealand, thousands of miles from Great Britain, where he lived most of his life, and where he made the discoveries that revolutionized our understanding of the atom.

The colony of New Zealand consisted of two islands—the North Island, including the towns of Auckland and Wellington, and the South Island, where Christchurch was located. Once the land became an English colony, in 1741, people from Great Britain began to arrive. Many of them came from Scotland. Ernest's grandfather, George Rutherford, came from Scotland in 1843 aboard a 125-foot sailboat. The journey took more than six months.

George Rutherford was a wheelwright, a skilled handyman, and had been recruited by another colonist to set up a sawmill. His son, James Rutherford, who was five years old when the family arrived on the South Island, would also become a wheelwright. James was known for being able to make almost anything. As a boy, he made a bicycle entirely from wood.

Christchurch, New Zealand

Caroline Thompson, Ernest's grandmother, was born and raised in Sussex, England. Widowed at a young age, she emigrated to New Zealand in 1855 with her parents, three sons, and her thirteen-year-old daughter, Martha. The family settled near New Plymouth on the North Island, where Caroline began teaching school.

There was tension on the North Island between the Europeans and the native Maoris. To escape the conflict Caroline and her children had moved to the South Island. Eventually, Caroline remarried, and Martha began teaching school.

James and Martha Rutherford circa the 1880s

In 1866, Martha Thompson married James Rutherford. They lived at Spring Grove, later called Brightwater. On August 30, 1871, wintertime in New Zealand, Ernest, their fourth child, was born. James and Martha would have a total of twelve children.

In the late nineteenth century New Zealand was largely undeveloped. As a boy, Ernest spent much of his time outdoors, exploring forests, fishing, and bird-watching. The Rutherford children had daily chores, such as milking cows and feeding animals.

These were rough economic times in New Zealand, and the family had to make several moves so James could find work. When Ernest was five, they moved to Foxhill on the South Island, where James hoped to get work making railroad ties. He also built a flax mill and did any fix-it jobs needed by his neighbors.

The Rutherford family at Havelock circa the early 1880s. Left to right: Alice Rutherford, Mary Thompson (*cousin*), Arthur Rutherford (*in front*), Ernest Rutherford (*behind*), Eve Rutherford (*in front, wearing white*), James Rutherford (*seated in chair*), Nell Rutherford (*standing behind*), Ethel Rutherford (*in front, wearing white*), Flo Rutherford (*seated in chair*), George Rutherford (*immediately behind*), Herbert Rutherford (*at rear*), Martha Rutherford (*standing side on*), Charles Rutherford, and Jim Rutherford

The New Zealand Education Act provided free elementary schooling for children ages five to fifteen. When Ernest started school at Foxhill his schoolteacher mother had already taught him how to read and spell short words and the multiplication tables. She often told her children "all knowledge is power."

Ernest's first exposure to science was at Foxhill. His first science book had a preface that said, "This book has been written, not so much to give information, as to endeavour to discipline the mind by bringing it into immediate contact with Nature herself, for which purpose a series of simple experiments are described leading up to the chief truths of each science, so that the powers of observation in the pupils may be awakened and strengthened."

One experiment taught how to determine the distance one was from a cannon by counting the seconds between the flash of firing and the sound. Ernest used this method one night during a thunderstorm. He figured out how far away the storm was by counting the seconds between seeing the lightning and hearing the thunder.

A family story about Ern, as he was called, happened while he and Jim were bringing the cows home in the evening and gathering wood on a sledge— similar to a wagon body without wheels that was dragged along the ground. Ern's inspiration was to tie the wood laden sledge to a cow's tail and let her pull the load. The plan worked, until the sledge caught on a gate and the end of the cow's tail ripped off.

Ern liked to make things, much as his father did. Years

later his mother recalled, "At one time he had a passion for taking photographs of his family, brothers and sisters, with a home-made camera, and he was continually taking clocks to pieces. Reading was his great recreation."

Entertainment in the Rutherford household consisted of reading aloud, competitions on school work, and music. Martha played a Broadwood piano and James played the violin.

Rutherford's flax mill in Opunake, New Zealand, circa 1897

In 1881, the family moved to Havelock, where James built a flax mill. Flax was used to make rope and mats and only grows in swampy areas. James leased swamp land from the Maoris. A newspaper reporter wrote that he visited the mill and "Mr. Rutherford... informed us that he turns out from eight to ten tons of flax per week."

The schoolteacher in Havelock, Jacob Reynolds, made an impression on Ern. Reynolds taught Ern and his brother to stand tall and to look people in the eye. Even in the overcrowded classroom, he established discipline. Reynolds offered his best students extra time for lessons before school, and Ern participated.

A replica of Rutherford's childhood home on display at Founders Heritage Park in Nelson, New Zealand

On Sundays, the Rutherfords attended the Anglican church, where Ern learned his catechism and won a prize for the most memorized Bible verses. But, in later life, he was not religious.

His mother often asked Ern to teach his sisters. He would reply, "If they are mustered out by 9 o'clock, I will, but you must do the mustering." His sisters claimed that he kept them quiet and in place by tying their pigtails to the sister on each side.

In December 1885, Ern tested for a scholarship to provide free board and tuition at Nelson College. In their system, Nelson College would be comparable to high school today. Over two days, the applicants took tests morning and afternoon on English, arithmetic, English history, and geography. When the results were announced, Ern had come in second, so there would be no scholarship for him. Because he finished only fifteen points behind the winner, a member of the school board tried to convince the board to obtain a special scholarship for Ern. He was not successful, so Ern stayed one more year as Reynolds' student. Since he was fourteen, he had a few more months of free education under the Education Act.

In January 1886, summertime in New Zealand, a friend stopped by the Rutherford house to see if Ernest, Jim, and Herbert would go with him on a fishing trip in Hoods Bay. Ern had to work in the flax mill that day, so he didn't go. Jim, Herbert, and Charlie Rutherford went for the day. As one of Ern's sisters wrote the story to an aunt, after they had been sailing and fishing for a while, "the boat capsized & threw them in the water." They hung onto the boat for about two hours and then Charlie was knocked off when the boat flipped again and went under. Jim tried to get to him, but failed, and soon, Herbert also drowned. Jim and the other boys were rescued by people passing in another boat.

His sister remembered that her mother was playing the piano when Ern rushed in with the news that Charlie and Herbert had drowned. Her children said that she never played the piano again. The boys were only twelve and ten years old when they drowned. For several months, James Rutherford and his surviving sons searched along the shores of the Bay, but their bodies were never found. The reporter from the newspaper of the nearest town wrote, "Mr. and Mrs. Rutherford are much respected and this sad affair has cast quite a gloom over the whole district, and the two deceased lads were very much liked by their schoolfellows."

Soon after his fifteenth birthday, Ern took the Junior Civil Service examination. He thought that might be his route to a job since he had not gotten the Nelson scholarship. The two-day exam covered the same subjects as the scholarship test, but Ern did not do as well. Applicants who scored ahead of him had already been in secondary schools, and they scored higher. Still Ern's scores were good enough that a year later the New Zealand government invited him to join the Civil Service. But by then, Ern had other plans.

The scholarships for students were limited to those under fifteen, except in Marlborough Province, where Ern lived. Students from there were expected to be behind in school, so they were allowed to test for the scholarship up to age sixteen. So Ern got another chance.

When the results were posted, Ern had won the scholarship. He got a perfect score of two hundred in arithmetic, the highest score for English, and high enough in history and geography to win the scholarship. The school had a special ceremony to congratulate him and gave him five volumes of *The Peoples of the World*.

When Ernest entered Nelson College, there was a total of eighty students, from ten to twenty-one years old. As a boarder, Ernest lived in a dormitory with three other boys and attended classes taught by four teachers or masters. He also joined the Nelson College Cadet Corps, wearing a uniform and drilling with rifles.

William Littlejohn, from Scotland, was the master of math and science, and he had a big influence on Ernest. Littlejohn also coached rugby and cricket, and Ern played on the rugby team.

One of Ernest's classmates remembered an ability that he already had and that would serve him well in his professional life. "He had such powers of concentration that he would continue to read in the uproar of an unsupervised common-room, but when a missile landed on his head he would roar into activity with good-humoured rage."

At Nelson College, Ernest did well in all subjects with no indication that science would be his life. He later complimented Littlejohn by saying, "He was a fine teacher of mathematics. The boys varied in ability but he grounded them all thoroughly in algebra, Euclid [geometry] and mechanics." He also said, "the science teaching did not attract me so much, for I imagine Littlejohn had not the same width of knowledge in the subject as in mathematics."

The scholarship that Ernest had won to Nelson lasted for two years. He hoped to win entrance and a scholarship to the university at the end of that time. Littlejohn tutored him in the evenings, and Ernest spent hours at his books. Ten scholarships would be awarded from all of New Zealand. Ernest took the exams in December 1888. He scored high enough to be admitted to the university, but not for a scholarship. He decided to return to Nelson College for another year and then try again.

The two-year scholarship had ended, but his good grades brought money prizes that allowed him to stay a third year. He earned both a classics scholarship and a history scholarship the first year, bringing him a total of forty pounds.

For this third year, Ernest was top of the crowd, earning the title "head boy" or "Dux."

Ernest planned to take the test for the scholarship to the university, but he realized he needed a back-up plan. He applied to be a science teacher at a high school in New Plymouth. To receive a scholarship, Ernest had to make high grades in five subjects: Latin, English, French, mathematics, and science. An example of a question in the science portion: "Show that the velocity of sound in air is not affected by variations of pressure, but that it is affected by variations of temperature."

A week before the scholarship scores would come out, Ernest learned that he had not been chosen for the high school teacher position. A man with some teaching experience had gotten the job.

Finally, the scholarship numbers arrived. Ernest had scored a total of 3792 points out of a possible 5750, putting him in fourth place. He had won a scholarship to the university.

2

Off to Other Parts

F OR A BOY coming from the frontier, Christchurch, with a population of 50,000, was a big city. The distance was far enough from his family that he only returned home on the long summer holidays. Other holidays, he stayed with his grandmother or other relatives.

Canterbury College, Rutherford's school, was one part of the University of New Zealand. About three hundred students, both full time and part time, attended the college. There were a total of five professors.

Rutherford enrolled in the three-year program leading to a bachelor of arts degree. His courses were Latin, pure mathematics, French, and applied mathematics. He also took a Saturday morning class called physics for schoolteachers. For board, Rutherford and another student shared a room in a boardinghouse.

The College Science Society and the Dialectic [debate] Society were Rutherford's extracurricular activities. He stayed in the Dialectic Society for two years, but as a spectator, not a debater. At this time in his life, Rutherford was shy and usually quiet around strangers.

The original site of Canterbury
College is today the Art Centre
in Christchurch, New Zealand.

English Professor Brown assigned essays and expected his students to take extensive notes. The class was comprised of 164 students, squeezed into a room built for seventy. Rutherford already had strong grammar skills, his mother and Jacob Reynolds had seen to that, and for the rest of his life his writing remained clear and strong.

The Physical Science building was a two-story tin building, known as the Tin Shed or the "realm of stinks." Professor Alexander Bickerton, known as Bicky, taught the classes, including physics and chemistry. Three more professors taught the other subjects at Canterbury College.

Toward the end of the year, the Science Society sponsored a conversazione, or an open house, to demonstrate scientific principles and ideas. It was attended by other students and the public. Rutherford described a typical evening in a letter to his mother:

> The college hall was fixed with tables on which all sorts of scientific apparatus was exhibited—mirrors, electric trains, motors, batteries and every scientific appliance you could think of. I was boss of what they called the 'darkroom' in which I had to exhibit a good deal of apparatus.... They consisted of spectroscopes to show the spectra of solar light, light of a gas flame, candle etc, an electric fountain, fluorescent tubes, Geissler tubes, electromagnetic star driven by electricity. I had one of the students as assistant and managed to work the affair pretty well. It was rather dangerous work fixing the wires up in the dark as you might get a very nasty shock from the large induction coil I had there.... I explained my apparatus for about 3 hours before a continually changing audience.

In each of the three years that Rutherford spent at Canterbury College, he won honors and prize money that kept him at school. He needed the extra money to supplement his scholarship.

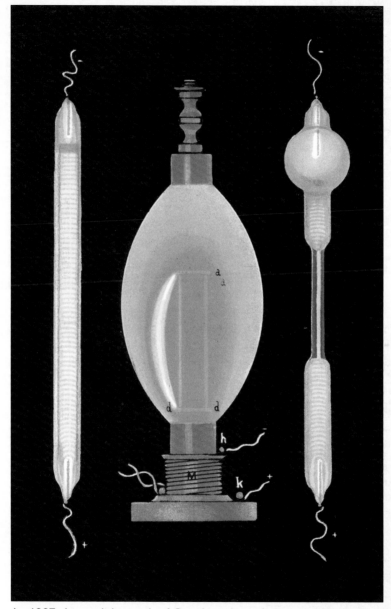

An 1887 chromolithograph of Geissler tubes, electron tubes used to study the behavior of gases

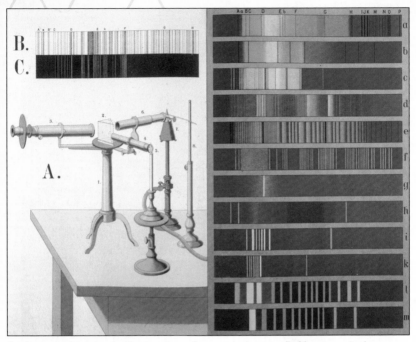

A nineteenth-century illustration of a spectroscope (left), an optical instrument used to analyze light, and a color chart (right)

In his second year, Rutherford enrolled in an experimental physics class taught by Bicky. Students learned about heat, light, and sound and used such instruments as thermometers, spectroscopes, induction coils, and batteries. Classes and experiments were conducted in the Tin Shed with equipment that had to be set up and taken down each time.

The next year, 1892, Rutherford was in honors physics. At the end of the year, he received a B. A. with first-class honors in physics.

Rutherford wished to return to Canterbury College the next year and took a scholarship exam again. He won a scholarship for his scores in math and mathematical physics and came back to study for the third year. At the end of 1893, Rutherford received a master of arts degree and earned first honors in both math and physics.

During his time at Christchurch [referred to by the initials ChCh in some letters], Rutherford began rooming with a widow named

Mary Newton. Her husband had died young of alcoholism and Newton had become an avid advocate of the temperance movement, which pushed for laws making alcoholic beverages illegal. She supported her four children by running a boardinghouse. Her daughter, Mary Georgina, was about five years younger than Rutherford. She was always called May to distinguish her from her mother. Before long, Rutherford was interested in May.

Alexander Bickerton circa 1878

Rutherford began to do research under the guidance of Bicky. He studied electricity and magnetism. In later years, he remembered that "I learnt more of research methods in those first investigations under somewhat difficult conditions than in any work I have done since."

At first, Rutherford tried to work in the Tin Shed or in a large commons area. Part of his experiments involved measurements with an instrument that was sensitive to vibrations. The instrument would react with footsteps or wind currents when someone opened a door. Bicky managed to scrounge some room for Rutherford to conduct his experiments. It was a basement room that Rutherford remembered as a "miserable, cold, draughty, concrete-floored cellar."

Working in this unsuitable place, Rutherford invented a timer that would switch electrical circuits in less than one-hundred-thousandth of a second. Then he moved on to other research.

In 1894, Rutherford returned to Canterbury College. He had no more scholarship, but he supported himself by tutoring students. He needed to be a student to apply for an overseas scholarship.

The scholarship also required original research. Rutherford had been considering a career in medicine, but he decided to stay with physics and try for the scholarship.

After reading papers about experiments on electrical currents in iron, Rutherford decided to investigate. The material he read included research on James Clerk Maxwell's theory of electromagnetism. Maxwell had discovered a set of equations that showed that electricity and magnetism are evidence of electromagnetic force. Maxwell was influenced by the earlier work of Michael Faraday, who had invented the dynamo and electromagnetic induction by producing an electrical current in wires turning inside a magnetic field. Based on the work of these two men, scientists believed that the depth that an iron bar was magnetized by an electrical current depended on how fast the current switched. The idea was that if the current changed too fast, there would be no magnetic field in the iron.

Rutherford's research refuted this idea. He proved that the "iron still keeps its magnetic properties for frequencies of 500 million."

A Marconi magnetic radio wave detector, nicknamed the "Maggie" and patented by Guglielmo Marconi in 1902. The action of all magnetic detectors is based on Rutherford's work.

The timer used to measure the experiments was from his first research. With the timer, he could detect the direction of current flowing in a millisecond. Even though his conclusions were not supported by famous scientists, Rutherford published his paper in 1894.

Part of his work involved inducing a magnetic field in a needle. Rutherford found that when a short burst of current induced the field, only a thin layer of the outside of the needle was magnetized. He measured this layer by monitoring the magnetic field as the needle was dissolving in a beaker of boiling, dilute nitric acid.

James Maxwell

He also began to experiment with radio waves. Just ten years before, Heinrich Hertz had detected waves that had been predicted by Maxwell's equations. Rutherford invented a device that would send and detect radio signals through sixty feet of a building. No one had yet developed radios as we know today, but being able to detect the faint signals was a breakthrough.

As he finished his research and began writing his papers, another opportunity came to Rutherford—he became a substitute math teacher for a high school. One of his students later recalled, "He was entirely hopeless as a school master. Disorder prevailed in his classes....We certainly had him added up as a genial person whose interests were nothing to do with the keeping in order of small boys."

Rutherford's main aim in this year was to win the Exhibition of 1851 Scholarship. In 1851, the Great Exhibition had been held in London as a display of industry and science. It was proposed by Prince Albert, the Prince Consort, husband of Queen Victoria, who was always interested in scientific and technological advances.

Over six months, exhibits from around Great Britain and other countries had been on view, and the Exhibit was a huge success. The profits were used to establish museums and to fund scholarships for students from Great Britain, Ireland, Canada, Australia, and New Zealand. Students would be awarded 150 pounds per year and could use the money to study anywhere they wanted in the British Empire.

Professor Bickerton wrote a recommendation for Rutherford: "From the first he exhibited an unusual aptitude for experimental science and in research work showed originality and capacity of a high order... Mr. Rutherford conducted a long and important investigation in the time effects of electrical and magnetic phenomena in rapidly alternating fields, and by means of an ingenious apparatus of his own design, was enabled to measure and observe phenomena occupying less than 1/100,000th of a second." Bicky added, "Personally Mr. Rutherford is of so kindly a disposition and so willing to help other students over their difficulties that he has endeared himself to all who have been brought into contact with him."

While waiting on the results for the Exhibition Scholarship, Bicky encouraged Rutherford to submit his research to the *Transactions of the New Zealand Institute*. Bicky wrote a letter to the editor and the editor replied, "Of course Rutherford's papers will be printed if sent up through the Society. I glanced over his theses before posting it to London. It seemed very high class work."

When the award of the Exhibition of 1851 Scholarship was announced Rutherford had come in second. A chemist, J. C. Maclaurin, had beat him out. Maclaurin had researched using cyanide in the separation of gold from ores. Newspapers in New Zealand carried the news, "The Science Scholarship awarded to Mr. J. Maclaurin B. Sc. of Auckland. Mr. Rutherford of Christchurch came in second."

However, fate was on Rutherford's side. Maclaurin had recently married and when he learned about the terms of the scholarship, he realized that it was not enough for him and his wife to live on in England. The rules specified that a recipient was required to be engaged in research full time and could not take on an extra job. Maclaurin turned down the scholarship. His sponsor, Professor Brown, wrote to the scholarship committee protesting this arrangement. "The fact is that the conditions of the Scholarship do not meet the wants of Auckland students who, very generally, have to earn their own living even while attending the College classes."

A cable was sent to London—"Maclaurin declines. Can you recommend Rutherford." The answer came back—"Certainly."

As Rutherford told a friend later, he was digging potatoes in the family vegetable garden when his mother ran out with the telegram that announced he was awarded the Exhibition of 1851 Scholarship. Rutherford threw down his shovel and said, "That's the last potato I will ever dig."

On August 1, 1895, Rutherford boarded a steamer to England. When the ship made a stop in Australia, Rutherford was able to meet W. H. Bragg, another scientist studying electromagnetic waves. They became good friends and corresponded regularly.

Rutherford and May Newton were unofficially engaged, but just as Maclaurin had learned, the scholarship was not large enough to support a wife. Rutherford and May would have to wait a few years before they married. During Rutherford's travels, May was often disappointed in the content of his letters. He replied, "I am afraid you will have to get accustomed to that sort for I don't naturally take to being very loving on paper."

At another stop, he wrote about a group of sightseers that he joined that included a woman. However, he wrote May, "The result of being in love with a particular young lady makes me rather critical of other ladies for naturally I have not seen anyone to compare with the aforementioned individual."

From Australia, the ship traveled across the Indian Ocean, through the Suez Canal into the Mediterranean Sea, and eventually through the straits of Gibraltar. Three weeks before they docked in England, Rutherford celebrated his twenty-fourth birthday.

Sir Joseph John Thomson working in the Cavendish Laboratory
at the University of Cambridge in England, 1904

3

New Rays and New Research

W HEN RUTHERFORD ARRIVED in England, on September 20, 1895, he received a letter of welcome from Sir J. J. Thomson, director of the Cavendish Laboratory of the Cambridge University.

> I shall be very glad for you to work at the Cavendish Laboratory and will give you all the assistance I can. Though it is not absolutely necessary, I think you will find it advantageous to become a member of the University. We have now instituted a degree for research so that anyone who resides for two years and does an original investigation, which receives the approval of the examiners, receives a degree...If you could spare the time to come to Cambridge for a few hours, I should be glad to talk matters over with you...I am much obliged to you for your paper, I hope to take an early opportunity of studying it.

Rutherford took a train to Cambridge and spent the day with Thomson. In a letter to May, he said, "The country is pretty enough but rather monotonous," and then went on to describe his visit with Thomson. "I went to the Lab and saw Thomson and had a good long talk with him. He is very pleasant in conversation and is not fossilized at all." Thomson took Rutherford home for lunch "where I saw his wife…very talkative and affable." Rutherford told May that Mrs. Thomson had tried to make him feel at home. He also described Thomson's three-year-old son as the "best little kid I have seen for looks and size." While Rutherford was in Cambridge, he often visited the Thomson's home.

Thomson at work in the Cavendish Laboratory

At lunch that day were three future Nobel Prize winners: Thomas Thomson for physics in 1906, George Paget Thomson for physics in 1937, and Ernest Rutherford for chemistry in 1908.

Rutherford decided to accept the post at the Cavendish Laboratory and moved to Cambridge. The Cavendish, which had been started in the same year that Rutherford was born, was the premier science institute in Great Britain.

The Cavendish building

As the first postgraduate at Cavendish who had received his degrees in New Zealand, Rutherford was an oddity to the other students. Most of the other postgraduates had got degrees at Cavendish. Rutherford socialized mostly with the few students who came from other schools. His best friend was the Irishman J. S. Townsend.

Some of the demonstrators, or what we would call lab instructors, resented the students from other places. For the first few months, Rutherford and Townsend were ignored. Another student who also became a scientist remembered:

> We ordinary Cambridge students...were inclined at first to look at a little askance at these representatives of a new species...We soon found, however that most of them fitted into the picture remarkably well. Rutherford was probably the most brilliant of them all though we might not have recognized him as such for ourselves. He was open and friendly in his manner...I think we young cynics might have described his manner as rather hearty and even a little boisterous, but I can imagine us allowing, with pride in our tolerance, that a man who had been reared on a farm somewhere on the outer fringes of the British Empire, might naturally be like that, and might nevertheless have the remarkable ability which rumour was beginning to attribute to him.

The animosity from the native students bothered Rutherford. He wrote that "many of them are my enemies...There is one demonstrator on whose chest I would like to dance a Maori war-dance."

But Rutherford continued on with his work. Eventually, the hard work and obvious intelligence earned him respect. Andrew Balfour, who became an expert on tropical diseases, said of Rutherford, "We've got a rabbit here from the Antipodes, and he's burrowing mighty deeply." Antipodes means the opposite side of the world, and for the British the term referred to Australia and New Zealand.

Rutherford was not always complimentary about the people in England. He wrote, "You can't imagine how slow-moving, slow-thinking the English villager is. He is very different to anything one gets hold of in the colonies."

Eventually, J. J. Thomson persuaded Rutherford to join a college to enhance his social and educational network. Rutherford chose Trinity College.

Rutherford had brought with him from New Zealand the device to detect wireless signals that he had built. Thomson later remembered that "Rutherford began his work at the Laboratory by working at wireless telegraphy, using a detector which he had invented before leaving New Zealand.... He held, not long after he had been at work in the Laboratory, the record for long-distance telegraphy, as he had succeeded in sending messages from the Laboratory to his rooms about three-quarters of a mile away."

Sir Robert Ball, director of the Cambridge University Observatory, heard about Rutherford's detector. He saw possibilities of using wireless signals at lighthouses. The lighthouse would transmit a wireless signal which would be detected by receivers on ships. The signals would help them to avoid rocks. Thomson also did some research to see if the device held commercial possibilities, and Rutherford wrote to May, "The reason I am so keen on the subject [of radio detection] is because of its practical importance.... If my next week's experiments come out as well as I anticipate, I see a chance of making cash rapidly in the future." Unfortunately, it wasn't feasible to promote the device commercially.

Thomson persuaded Rutherford to present his radio wave work to the Royal Society, the premier science organization in Britain. On June 18, 1896, Rutherford spoke about his research to the Society. His paper, "A Magnetic Detector of Electrical Waves and Some of Its Applications," was published in the Society's journal, *Philosophi-*

cal Transactions. Afterward, he and Thomson moved on to other projects.

Rutherford needed money. Even with the scholarship, supporting himself was difficult, and he still hoped to make enough money to marry May. Thomson helped him find extra income from tutoring, reviewing books, and administering exams.

For his first Christmas in England, Rutherford celebrated with a trip to Scotland. He wrote to May that he only saw the sun once during the whole holiday.

While Rutherford was spending Christmas in Scotland, a scientific paper was published that would send his life into a new direction.

Wilhelm Roentgen, a German physicist, was only one of the scientists around the world experimenting with cathode tubes: glass tubes with a positive terminal, the anode, at one end and the negative, the cathode, at the other. Earlier it had been revealed that when the tubes were partially evacuated of air, which allowed the electricity to flow from one end to the other, the tube would glow. But no one knew what caused the glow.

Roentgen wanted to learn more about the light, so he wrapped a cathode tube with cardboard and turned off the laboratory lights to make sure the cardboard was secure. Then he noticed that a nearby fluorescent

Wilhelm Roentgen

screen was shimmering. He concluded that some kind of rays coming from the end of the cathode tube had caused the effect. For several days, he investigated the rays. He named them x-rays, with x meaning unknown, as it is used in mathematical equations.

One of the most striking experiments with the new rays showed the bones of Mrs. Roentgen's hand and the ring on her finger. The mysterious rays had zoomed through the flesh and created an image of her bones.

J. J. Thomson was intrigued by these new rays, and he immediately set up his own experiments. As he wrote in the science journal, *Nature,* "The discovery by Professor Roentgen of the rays which bear his name has aroused an interest unparalleled in the history of physical science...experiments seems to show that these rays exert a powerful disintegrating effect on the molecules of substances through which they pass, and suggest that their use may throw light on some questions of molecular structure."

When J. J. asked his New Zealand student to work with him on the new rays, Rutherford

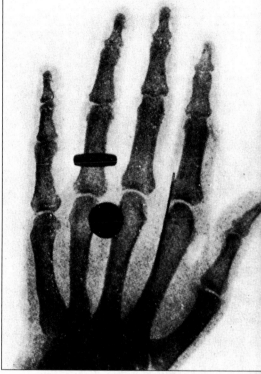

One of Roentgen's early x-ray images

was ready. He wrote that "I am a little full up of my old subject and am glad of a change. I expect it will be a good thing for me to work with the Professor for a time. I have done one research to show I can work by myself."

Rutherford and Thomson knew that scientists around the world were working on experiments similar to theirs. Rutherford wrote, "The professor of course is trying to find out the real cause and nature of the waves, and the great object is to find the theory of the matter before anyone else, for nearly every Professor in Europe is now on the warpath."

In experiments that Rutherford and Thomson carried out, they found that when x-rays pass through a gas, the gas becomes an insulator rather than a conductor of electricity. We know now that this is because the gas slowed down the exchange of electrons from one atom to another.

The experiments also revealed that cathode rays carried a negative charge and, by making a vacuum in the cathode tube, they demonstrated that the ray would bend in an electric field. The reason, according to Thomson, was "I can see no escape from the conclusion that [cathode rays] are charges of negative electricity carried by particles of matter." He wondered, "What are these particles? Are they atoms, or molecules, or matter in a still finer state of subdivision?"

Rutherford and Thomson theorized that the cathode rays were making ions, charged particles, out of gas molecules. When someone stated that ions might not exist, Rutherford is said to have replied that he was sure of their existence: "jolly little beggars, so real that I can almost see them." His strong ability to visualize even the atomic realm was one of Rutherford's strengths.

In 1897, Thomson performed the experiment that made his name famous. Continuing with the experiments on x-rays in cathode tubes, he measured the mass-to-charge ratio, m/e, for the ions. He found that either the mass was very small or the charge was extremely large. Other experiments showed that the mass was much smaller than that of an atom. Thomson had discovered the electron.

Up until then it was assumed by most scientists that the atom could not be divided. The word *atom* itself comes from a Greek word meaning uncuttable. Now Thomson was proposing that there were smaller, negatively charged particles in the atom.

In the meantime, French scientist Henri Becquerel had discovered that a sample of uranium could emit rays even while being in a dark desk drawer. He theorized that it was a different kind of ray than the x-rays others were studying.

A hand-colored photograph of Henri Becquerel in his laboratory

Marie and Pierre Curie in their laboratory, circa 1905

Marie and Pierre Curie, also in France, refined uranium ore, pitchblende, and measured the rays coming from different parts. Marie named the phenomenon radioactivity, from the word for ray. She and Pierre discovered two new elements, polonium and radium, in their pile of uranium ore. Marie also found that the rays coming from uranium did not depend on the state of the uranium. Rays were produced by solid or powdered uranium and also when it was combined with other atoms in molecules. This led her to conclude that the rays must be a property of the atom.

Rutherford turned to researching the rays being emitted by uranium. He discovered two different rays. One had a positive charge and did not travel far from the source. He named it alpha radiation. Today, we know that alpha rays are helium ions. The second ray, Rutherford named beta. It  has a negative charge and travels farther than the alpha ray. We now know it is an electron. Later, Rutherford found another very energetic ray which a fellow scientist named gamma. Alpha, beta, and gamma are the first three letters of the Greek alphabet. In his autobiography, Thomson praised Rutherford's work, saying, "Rutherford ... investigated the radiation from uranium very thoroughly. He found that the radiation was of two types, one type, which he called the alpha  type, being absorbed after passing through a few millimeters of air, while the other, the beta type, could get through more than twenty times this distance."

By this time, Rutherford's two-year Exhibition of 1851 Scholarship was about to run out. Thomson recommended that he apply for a third year and wrote to the commissioners that Rutherford "is quite in the first rank of physicists.... If it is not contrary to the rules to renew his Scholarship, I am sure such a proceeding would tend greatly to the advancement of Physical Science." The recommendation worked, and Rutherford received money for two more years. However, he would not stay at the Cavendish the entire time.

May came to England for a visit in 1897. She attended the ceremony when Rutherford received his B.A. from Cambridge University. But he was  still not making enough money for them to marry. Soon, an opportunity from Canada would change their circumstances.

The Greek letters alpha, beta, and gamma

4

McGill and Montreal

IN THE AUTUMN OF 1898 officials from McGill University in Montreal, Canada, came to England to look for someone to chair their physics department. When they asked J. J. Thomson who he would recommend, he said Rutherford. As he had in his recommendation for extending Rutherford's scholarship, Thomson praised his work. "I have never had a student with more enthusiasm or ability for original research than Mr. Rutherford and I am sure that if elected he would establish a distinguished school of Physics at Montreal. I should consider any Institution fortunate that secured the services of Mr. Rutherford as a Professor of Physics."

Rutherford was excited at the possibility of chairing the department. He felt his chances of advancement at Cambridge were limited. In spite of his groundbreaking work with radiation, he had not been made a fellow of his college. Fellowships were usually awarded to the top students of the postgraduates, but as Rutherford wrote to May, "As far as I can see my chances for a Fellowship are very slight. All the dons practically and naturally dislike very much the idea of

A late nineteenth-century photo of Old Hall, the oldest standing building at McGill University in Montreal, Canada one of us getting a Fellowship, and no matter how good a man is, he will be chucked out...I think it would be much better for me to leave Cambridge, on account of the prejudice of the place, I know perfectly well that if I had gone through the regular Cambridge course, and done a third of the work I have done, I would have got a Fellowship bangoff....One has to face the situation squarely and not look always on the rosy side."

May probably would have liked Rutherford to come back to New Zealand, but he told her, "my chances of advancement are much better in McGill, than if I got out to New Zealand."

He wrote May that, although he might not get the appointment, if he did he would "have to start work at once, so the question is what am I going to do when my vacation arrives. Am I to go to New Zealand to fetch you to look after me and become Mrs. Professor, or am I to wait another year to get enough cash to do it in style?" The decision, he wrote, would depend on his schedule and the amount of money he would receive.

Then, on August 3, 1898, Rutherford was able to write a happy letter to May. "Rejoice with me, my dear girl, for matrimony is looming in the distance. I got word on Monday...to say I was appointed to Montreal." He still needed to repay money borrowed from his family for his trip to England, but then his salary at McGill would be enough to support a wife. He planned to teach a term and then travel to New Zealand during the summer vacation.

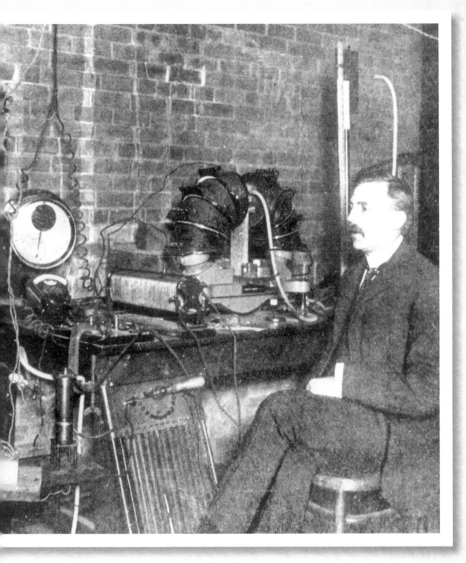

Rutherford in his lab at McGill in 1905

When talking about the work ahead, Rutherford said, "I am expected to do a lot of original work and to form a research school in order to knock the shine out of the Yankees! The physical laboratory is one of the best buildings of its kind in the world and has a magnificent supply of apparatus."

He had some qualms about being in charge of the place. "It sounds rather comic to myself to have to supervise the research of other men, but I hope I will get along all right. There are about four men doing research in the Lab, some of whom are as old as myself, so I will have to carry it off."

When Rutherford left England he was headed to one of the best outfitted labs in the world. When the Macdonald Physics Building (MPB) at McGill University opened in 1893 it was the most expensive physics lab in the world. The financier, Sir William Macdonald, made his money selling tobacco to Union soldiers during the American Civil War. In a paradox, he was against smoking, and the scientists in the lab always avoided smoking around him. Rutherford smoked a pipe, and many around him said he looked like a volcano at times. But when Macdonald visited, the pipe was hidden away, and windows were opened to blow away the smoke.

Rutherford's duties at McGill were heavy on research and light on teaching. That made it a good fit. While lecturing he was prone to go off on a tangent and to stray into subjects over the students' heads. His department chairman, John Cox, once had to remind him, "Calculus is fine in its place, a useful thing to know. But don't you think, that it is going too far to expect students who have not yet studied calculus to be able to apply it to physics."

When he arrived at McGill, Rutherford wrote to May, "I am very pleased with the Physics Building which is very large and fine … and filled with apparatus. Everything is very bright and polished, in fact, almost too much so for a building where work is to be done."

Before leaving England, Rutherford had ordered rare samples of uranium and thorium so he could continue his radioactivity research. When they arrived, he began experiments with the radioactive elements. He described what he called an "emanation" coming from the thorium. He could capture it in glass tubes that also became radioactive. He assumed that the "emanation" was a gas because of its actions, but he couldn't prove it because its radioactivity waned very fast.

Ernest Rutherford (front right) and colleagues outside the physics building at McGill University in 1906

This discovery intrigued Rutherford and he set out to learn more. He wrote May, "My dear girl, I keep going steadily turning to the Lab. Five nights out of seven, till 11 or 12 o'clock."

In a paper published by the *Philosophical Magazine,* in January 1900, Rutherford described the phenomenon: "In addition to this ordinary radiation (from thorium) I have found that thorium compounds continuously emit radioactive particles of some kind, which retain their radioactive powers for several minutes. This 'emanation' as it will be called for shortness, has the power of ionizing the gas in its neighbourhood and of passing through thin layers of metals, and, with great ease, through considerable thicknesses of paper."

Before Rutherford could investigate the phenomenon further he had to return to New Zealand to be married. May wrote to Ernest's mother: "Mother is writing to ask you to come down and see Ernest and myself married. Of course it will be only a very short and comparatively uninteresting affair as there will be no guests beyond my grandmother, Uncle Tom, and Uncle Sam and his wife and my mother and brothers and Mr. Rutherford and yourself and George whom Ernest is asking to be his best man.... We are going away for a short trip and then after ten days in ChCh [Christchurch] to pack and say goodbye to all my friends, we will come up to you, for ten days or so, if you will have us."

The couple was finally married on June 28, 1900. While in New Zealand, Rutherford also received a doctorate from the University of New Zealand.

By the time the Rutherfords arrived in Montreal, May was pregnant. Their only child, Eileen, was born at the end of March, 1901. Rutherford wrote to his mother, "You have probably been aware for several days that you have now the honour of being a grandmother. I hope Father feels correspondingly dignified after reaching the stage of grandfather.

Rutherford and his wife, Mary Georgina, in 1937

The baby much to Mary's delight, is a she, and is apparently provided with the usual number of limbs.... The baby is of course a marvel of intelligence and we think there was never such a fine baby before."

Besides marriage, Rutherford entered into another partnership. Frederick Soddy was a chemist at McGill University who had recently arrived from Oxford, England. He came with hopes of being made a chemistry professor, but the job had been given to someone else.

Frederick Soddy

The men solidified their partnership at a debate before the Physical Society during which Rutherford and Soddy disagreed about the structure of the atom.

Rutherford, as chairman of the Society, had chosen as a topic for the evening, "The existence of bodies smaller than an atom" and Soddy presented an opposition paper entitled, "Chemical evidence of the indivisibility of the atom." In his paper, Soddy attacked Rutherford's position with strong words: "Recent advances connected with the discovery of the cathode, Rontgen and Becquerel types of radiation have led physicists to the belief that in these phenomena they are dealing with particles of matter smaller by a thousand times than the absolute mass of the atom. So certain are they of the interpretation of their experimental results and of the inability of the present hypotheses to explain them that not a few of them have definitely abandoned the accepted notion of the structure of matter and have boldly attacked the atomic theory which as everyone knows has been the foundation of chemistry as a science from the time of Dalton to the present day."

Soddy went on to accuse physicists of making assumptions to fit what they thought they saw in their experiments.

At the end of his paper, Soddy acknowledged Rutherford's work. "Possibly Professor Rutherford may be able to convince us that matter as known to him is really the same matter as known to us, or possibly he may admit that the world in which he deals is a new world demanding a chemistry and physics of its own, and in either case I feel sure chemists will retain a belief in, and a reverence for, atoms as concrete and permanent entities, if not immutable, certainly not yet transmuted."

Soddy's words were prophetic. In a matter of months the concept of transmutation would grow out of a collaboration between him and Rutherford, who soon after the debate invited Soddy to study the thorium "emanation" with him.

They started investigating together in October 1901 and worked as a team until early 1903, when Soddy returned to England. Their goal was to measure the speed and mass of the "emanations" emitted by radioactive thorium.

Their first task was collecting enough "emanation" to experiment with. When they had isolated enough, Soddy was able to determine that it was a gas belonging to the argon family. This set of gases had been discovered in 1894 and been given the name argon, or inert.

While Soddy studied the chemistry of the "emanation," Rutherford scrutinized its physical properties. When a negatively charged metal plate was exposed to it, the plate became radioactive, which meant the "emanation" was attracted to the negative plate because of a positive charge. Rutherford asked himself if this was the same alpha ray that he had discovered earlier.

Henri Becquerel and Sir William Crookes had discovered that the radioactivity of uranium salts could be deactivated by chemical reaction. When barium chloride was added to a uranium solution and the barium then precipitated with sulfate, the barium sulfate became radioactive and the activity of the uranium decreased to almost nothing. But as time passed, the uranium regained radioactivity and the barium lost it. Crookes called the precipitate Uranium X.

Rutherford and Soddy tried this experiment with thorium instead of uranium and found the same thing occurred. After two days, the thorium had recovered half of its activity and thorium X had lost half.

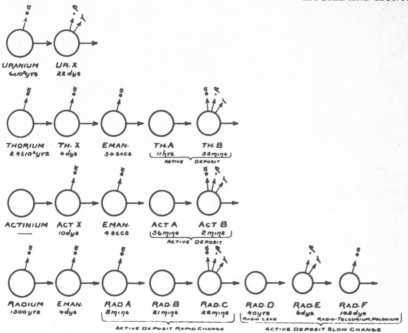

A diagram of the radioactive elements and their family of products from Rutherford's *Radioactive Transformations*

In his book, *Radio-activity,* written about these experiments, Rutherford stated that he came to two conclusions.

"(1) That there is a constant rate of production of fresh radio-active matter by the radio-active body;

(2) That the activity of the matter so formed decreases according to an exponential law with the time from the moment of its formation."

Uranium had a longer time frame of twenty-two days to regain half of its activity. These experiments led Rutherford and Soddy to state the rule that we call the half-life of a radioactive element. The half-life is the time required for one-half of the radioactivity to disappear. Different elements have different half-lives. The most common type of uranium has a long half-life of 4.5 billion years; the half-life of thorium is 24 days.

Rutherford and Soddy had discovered the concept of half-life, but their experiments were heading toward new ideas that would revolutionize chemistry and physics even more.

5

Transmutation?

THE EXPERIMENTS PERFORMED by Rutherford and Soddy pointed them toward a conclusion that did not fit current scientific belief. In ancient times, men had believed that they could find a way to convert one element into another; turn lead into gold. The process was called transmutation. Those who searched for this miraculous method were called alchemists. The alchemists failed, and scientists eventually concluded that one element could not be turned into another.

But in Rutherford and Soddy's experiments it appeared that the element thorium was turning into another element, thoron. As the implications became clear, Soddy said, "Rutherford, this is transmutation; the Thorium is disintegrating and transmuting itself into an argon gas."

"For Mike's sake, Soddy, don't call it transmutation," Rutherford said. "They'll have our heads off as alchemists.... Make it transformation."

When word of this groundbreaking discovery began to leak out to the other professors at McGill, some thought Rutherford's conclusions

A fourteenth-century painting
of an alchemist's equipment

would bring criticism and discredit to the university because his theory of transmutation was so radical. But most of the faculty and administration were supportive. John Cox, Rutherford's chairman, predicted "that the development of radioactivity would bring a renown to McGill University by which in the future it would be widely known abroad." Cox also predicted that "some day Rutherford's experimental work would be rated as the greatest since that of Faraday."

John McNaughton, a classics professor, often referred to scientists as plumbers, deriding their work. He visited Rutherford's laboratory on a tour of the campus and wrote an article for the campus newspaper saying, "we had stumbled in upon one of Dr. Rutherford's brilliant demonstrations of radium. It was indeed an eye-opener. The lecturer himself seemed like a large piece of the expensive and marvelous substance he was describing.... Here was the rarest and most refreshing spectacle—the pure ardour of the chase, a man quite possessed by a noble work and altogether happy in it."

Rutherford was often described as boisterous, loud, and rambunctious. Co-workers knew that he could explode in anger if something was broken or destroyed. But he also would sing when experiments were humming along. Usually the song he sang was "Onward, Christian Soldiers," sung off key but loud.

Rutherford and Soddy knew they were not the only ones investigating radioactive substances. Rutherford wrote to his mother in 1902, "I have to keep going as there are always people on my track. I have to publish my present work as rapidly as possible in order to keep in the race. The best sprinters in this road of investigation are Becquerel and the Curies in Paris who have done a great deal of very important work in the subject of radioactive bodies during the last few years." However, in the spirit of international cooperation, Marie Curie gave Rutherford a sample of radium to use in his experiments at McGill.

In experiments with thorium, radium, and uranium, Rutherford began to suspect that the release of radioactivity changed the atoms into other atoms. In the disintegration of a thorium atom, an atom of the also unstable element thoron, or as Rutherford called it at the time, Thorium-X, was formed. As Rutherford said, "To put it bluntly, thorium was an element, thorium-X another, and the atoms of thorium must be steadily transmuting themselves into atoms of thorium-X. No other conclusion was possible."

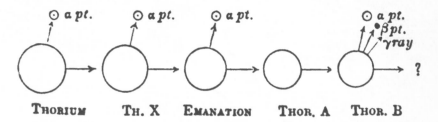

A diagram of the family of Thorium products from *Radioactive Transformations*

Rutherford and Soddy discovered a series of disintegrations, starting with radioactive elements and ending with stable elements such as lead. They called the original radioactive element, the "parent," and the subsequent elements the "daughters." For example, the radium and polonium discovered by the Curies were daughters of the parent element uranium.

When the radioactive elements disintegrated, alpha, beta, and gamma particles were released. No one yet knew exactly what these particles were, but Rutherford would have a hand in the determination of their identity.

So Rutherford and Soddy, in a short time of eighteen months, had blasted apart two of the foundations of chemistry: one, that atoms were indivisible, and two, that elements could not be transformed into other elements. Soddy later claimed, "By the time our cooperation ended, radioactivity, which had already become a considerable jigsaw puzzle, had been put together, and my chief impression of those days remains of an intense mental exaltation as the pieces came together and they were fitted by a single theory of atomic disintegration into a convincing whole."

In early 1903, Frederick Soddy left McGill to work in England. He eventually won the Nobel Prize in 1921 in chemistry for work he did after he left Canada.

Rutherford published a book about their discoveries. *Radioactivity* was first published in 1904, but new discoveries were happening so quickly a revised version came out the next year. Rutherford dedicated the book to his former professor, J. J. Thomson, "A tribute of my respect and admiration."

The first paragraph of the book states the groundbreaking nature of its contents: "The close of the old and the beginning of the new century have been marked by a very rapid increase of our knowledge of that most important but comparatively little known subject—the connection between electricity and matter.... The study of the radio-active substances and of the discharge of electricity through gases has supplied very strong experimental evidence in support of the fundamental ideas of the existing atomic theory. It has also indicated that the atom itself is not the smallest unit of matter, but is a complicated structure made up of a number of smaller bodies."

In the book, Rutherford described alpha, beta, and gamma particles and their activities. He showed how he and Soddy had developed the idea of half-life and the concept of the parent-daughter series. The fact that radioactivity could not be changed by physical or chemical forces indicated that "the cause of the disruption of the atoms of the radio-elements [radioactive elements] and their products resides in the atoms themselves."

Rutherford also spoke of the tremendous amounts of energy bound up in atoms. "There is thus reason to believe that there is an enormous store of latent energy resident in the atoms of the radio-elements." He also wrote, "there is no reason to assume that this enormous store of energy is possessed by the radio elements alone." Other non-radioactive elements would also have huge amounts of energy tied up in their atoms.

According to one biographer, Rutherford made two jokes about the energy bound up in an atom: "Could a proper detonator be found, it's just conceivable that a wave of atomic disintegration might be started through matter which would indeed make this old world vanish in smoke" and "Some fool in a laboratory might blow up the universe unawares."

In today's world, we understand more about the energy bound up in atoms. That energy is released in atomic bombs and provides the heat to power nuclear plants.

Uranium ore (left) and lead ore. Ore is mined from the earth and then processed to extract elements such as uranium and lead.

One of the corollaries of the radioactivity theory and half-life concept was that it could be used to estimate the age of the earth. Since radioactive elements in the rocks of the earth have been decaying at a steady rate, the half-life could be used to decipher the time since the earth's formation. For example, if the amounts of the parent, radioactive uranium and the amounts of the daughter, stable lead are equal, the rock must be one uranium half-life old, or 4.5 billion years.

Items other than rocks can be dated by using the half-life. All living things absorb a radioactive carbon known as carbon-14. When the organism dies it stops absorbing carbon-14. By measuring the amount of remaining carbon-14 and calculating the half-life scientists can make good determinations of the age of the mummy, fibers, or plant remains.

Rutherford also believed that the heat of the earth could be partially explained by the energy released when uranium decays into radium because emitted alpha rays release part of their energy as heat.

After *Radio-activity* was published, Rutherford began to receive job offers from prestigious universities in the United States, including Columbia and Yale. But at that time, research facilities in the U.S. were inferior to those in England, and Rutherford longed to return to Britain.

In 1903 Rutherford was accepted as a Fellow of the Royal Society (FRS), the highest science honor in Britain. He was invited to give that year's Bakerian Lecture for the Royal Society. In the lecture he discussed his theory of radioactivity. Later that year, he was awarded the Rumsford Medal of the Royal Society, given "to the author of the most important discovery or useful improvement which shall be made . . . during the preceding two years . . . the preference always being given to such discoveries as . . . tend most to promote the good of mankind."

A 1900 engraving of Lord Kelvin

While in England, he also spoke at the Royal Institution, the other prestigious science organization. The goal of the Royal Institution was "diffusing science for the common purposes of life." One of the members of the Royal Institution was the grand master British scientist of the day, eighty-year-old Lord Kelvin. Kelvin had investigated the heat of the earth and estimated the age of the planet to be 20 to 40 million years old. Rutherford's theory refuted that idea.

He had stated in *Radio-activity* that "there was an *internal* source supplying heat; and therefore the earth was not simply a cooling mass, and Kelvin's results did not hold."

Kelvin was in the audience when Rutherford gave his address. He later remembered:

> I came into the room, which was half dark, and presently spotted Lord Kelvin in the audience and realized that I was in for trouble at the last part of my speech dealing with the age of the earth, where my views conflicted with his. To my relief, Kelvin fell fast asleep, but as I came to the important point, I saw the old bird sit up, open an eye and cock a baleful glance at me! Then a sudden inspiration came, and I said Lord Kelvin had limited the age of the earth, *provided no new source was discovered.* That prophetic utterance refers to what we are now considering tonight, radium! Behold! The old boy beamed upon me.

Just as students had flocked to Cavendish Laboratory to be associated with J. J. Thomson, researchers now clamored to work with Rutherford at McGill. One student, Otto Hahn, came from Germany to study with Rutherford. Hahn spoke of Rutherford's regard for his students: "Rutherford was so sincere and unassuming in his dealing with his students and with everyday things of life....We had no doubt imagined that such a distinguished professor would be an unapproachable person, conscious of his dignity. Nothing could have been farther from the truth. I still possess a small photograph which shows him clearing away the snow from the entrance to his house."

When a photographer came to Rutherford's laboratory for a formal picture, he was not impressed with the professor's appearance. He requested that Rutherford borrow Hahn's white cuffs so he would look more dignified in the photograph.

Hahn went on to win the 1944 Nobel Prize for chemistry for the work he did with Lise Meitner that led to the discovery of nuclear fission.

The Rutherfords took a trip to Europe in 1903. They traveled to Paris so May could meet Ernest's friend, Paul Langevin, whom he had known at Cavendish. While there Rutherford met with other scientists as well.

The day they arrived, June 25, 1903, was also the day Marie Curie received her doctorate degree. As Rutherford later remembered:

> My old friend, Professor Langevin, invited my wife and myself and the Curies and Perrin to dinner. After a very lively evening, we retired about 11 o'clock in the garden, where Professor Curie brought out a tube coated in part with zinc sulphide and containing a large quantity of radium in solution. The luminosity was brilliant in the darkness and it was a splendid finale to an unforgettable day. At the time we could not help observing that the hands of Professor Curie were in a very inflamed and painful state due to exposure to radium rays.

At one point in the evening, Rutherford turned to Marie and said that radioactivity was "a splendid subject to work on." She agreed.

Early researchers did not fully understand the effects of radioactivity on the body. Marie Curie died of leukemia in 1934. Rutherford often carried rocks of radioactive ore, pitchblende, in his pocket, but appears to not have suffered consequences from his exposure.

In the next few years, Pierre replicated Rutherford's experiments. At first, he did not agree with Rutherford's conclusions about the "emanations" coming from the inside of the atom. But in 1904, Pierre published a paper, "adopting Mr. Rutherford's manner of seeing." Pierre Curie was killed in an accident two years later, but Marie and Rutherford corresponded for years.

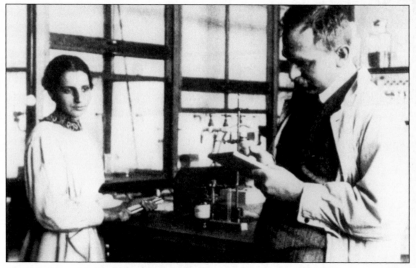

Otto Hahn with Lise Meitner in Hahn's laboratory in 1913

In 1906, Rutherford was invited to Philadelphia. He also planned on touring the United States. He wrote his mother, "I go to Philadelphia to attend the bicentenary of Franklin [Benjamin Franklin]. I am giving an address there. I hear this morning that the University of Philadelphia intend to confer on me the honorary degree of Doctor of Laws....I am rather youthful for such honours."

After the celebration in Philadelphia, Rutherford traveled to Berkeley, California, where he saw the results of the giant earthquake and fire that hit the area three months earlier. "It is certainly a most depressing sight. For miles there is nothing but heaps of bricks and tangled ironwork. Wooden buildings are going up everywhere for temporary use."

After the visit to California, Rutherford enjoyed another American sight—the Grand Canyon. "I am staying at the El Tovar Hotel right at the edge of the Grand Canyon of Arizona. The hotel is located right on the edge and you look twelve miles across a mass of peaks of sandstone and rocks of various colours left like battlements and castles 3000 to 6000 feet above the level of the Colorado ravine....The colours are very beautiful."

E. Rutherford

6

Winning the Nobel

I N SPITE OF the excellent laboratory and many outstanding students at McGill University, Rutherford felt out of touch with the scientific community in Montreal. He yearned to return to England. In 1906, he got an intriguing offer. Professor Arthur Schuster from the University of Manchester was retiring. He wrote to Rutherford, "I have not mentioned the matter to anyone in Manchester yet and I should like you to treat it as quite confidential. But any further steps would be made much easier if I could feel you were ready to step in should a vacancy occur. I really do not know of anyone else to whom I would care to hand over the office."

The lab at Manchester was not as good as the one at McGill, but it was superior to the facilities at the Cavendish. Manchester had been the home of prominent scientists, including John Dalton and James Prescott Joule. Rutherford wrote back to Schuster, "The fine laboratory you have built up is a great attraction to me as well as the opportunity of more scientific intercourse than occurs here." He agreed to become head of the physics department after finishing the school year at McGill.

A 1907 illustration of Rutherford at the Cavendish Laboratory in Cambridge

In his resignation from McGill, Rutherford stated that "the determining factor...[is]...my feeling that it is necessary to be in closer contact with European science than is possible on this side of the Atlantic."

Rutherford's entry to the academic world of the University of Manchester was loud. At the first science faculty meeting he attended, he was introduced and then strode to the podium and smashed his hand down, exclaiming "By thunder!"

Before Rutherford arrived to take over the physics department, the head of the chemistry department had moved some of his teachers and equipment into rooms that had previously been assigned to the physics department. Rutherford regained use of the rooms and soon set up his radioactivity experiments in them.

The Old Quadrangle at the University of Manchester in England

One of Rutherford's colleagues at Manchester was chemistry instructor Chaim Weizmann, who later became the first president of Israel. Weizmann said of Rutherford, "Youthful, energetic, boisterous, he suggested anything but the scientist. He talked readily and vigorously on any subject under the sun, often without knowing anything about it. Going down to the refectory for lunch, I would hear the loud, friendly voice rolling up the corridor. He was quite devoid of any political knowledge or feelings, being entirely taken up with his epoch making scientific work....Rutherford was modest, simple and enormously good natured."

Weizmann also became friends with another famous scientist, Albert Einstein. He contrasted the two with the statement:

> I have retained the distinct impression that Rutherford was not terribly impressed by Einstein's work, while Einstein on the other hand always spoke to me of Rutherford in the highest terms calling him a second Newton. As scientists the two men were strongly contrasting types—Einstein all calculation, Rutherford all experiment.... But there is no doubt that as an experimenter Rutherford was a genius, one of the greatest. He worked by intuition and whatever he touched turned to gold. He seemed to have a sixth sense in his tackling of experimental problems. Einstein achieved all his results by sheer calculation.

Rutherford knew that his work with radioactive elements and transmutation was worthy of a Nobel Prize. He wrote May that "If I am to have a chance for a Nobel Prize in the next few years I must keep my work moving." The big surprise was that he received the 1908 Nobel Prize in chemistry instead of physics. The Nobel citation said it was awarded to Rutherford "for his investigations into the disintegration of the elements, and the chemistry of radioactive substances."

As word of the award leaked out before the official notice, Rutherford received a congratulatory letter from his former student, Otto Hahn. Rutherford replied, "I must confess it was very unexpected and I am very startled at my metamorphosis into a chemist." Rutherford considered himself a physicist only and even was known to claim that "all science is either physics or stamp collecting."

Staff and students at the University of Manchester were thrilled to have a Nobel Prize winner in their midst. One made up a song about the achievement.

A ALPHA RAY

Air: 'A Jovial Monk.'

1. A alpha ray was I, contented with my lot;
From Radium C
I was set free,
And outwards I was shot.
My speed I quickly reckoned,
As I flew off through space,
Ten thousand miles per second
Is not a trifling pace!
For an alpha ray
Goes a good long way
In a short time t,
As you easily see;
Though I don't know why
My speed's so high,
Or why I bear a charge 2e.

4. But now I'm settled down, and move about quite slow;
For I, alas,
Am helium gas
Since I got that dreadful blow,
But though I'm feeling sickly,
Still no one now denies,
That I ran that race so quickly,
I've won a Nobel Prize.
For an alpha ray
Is a thing to pay,
And a Nobel Prize
One cannot despise,
And Rutherford
Has greatly scored,
As all the world now recognize.

The Rutherfords traveled to Stockholm, Sweden, for the ceremony. The award was presented on December 11, 1908, by the king of Sweden. The speech given during the presentation of the Nobel stated that "Rutherford's discoveries led to the highly surprising conclusion, that a chemical element, in conflict with every theory hitherto advanced, is capable of being transformed into other elements, and thus in a certain way it may be said that the progress of investigation is bringing us back once more to the transmutation theory propounded and upheld by the alchemists of old."

In speaking of the reason for the award being the chemistry prize: "Though Rutherford's work has been carried out by a physicist and with the aid of physical methods, its importance for chemical investigation is so far-reaching and

King Gustav V of Sweden

self-evident, that the Royal Academy of Sciences has not hesitated to award to its progenitor the Nobel Prize designed for original work in the domain of chemistry—thus affording a new proof to be added to the numerous existing ones, of the intimate interplay one upon another of the various branches of natural science in modern times."

In a letter home, May described the banquet held after the ceremonies and a toast to Ernest's health. "Everyone says he [Rutherford] made the speech of the evening and was rather amusing. He said he had dealt for a long time in transformations of varying length but that the quickest he had met was his own transformation in one moment from a physicist into a chemist!"

In his Nobel Lecture entitled "The Chemical Nature of the Alpha Particles from Radioactive Substances," Rutherford spoke about his work at Macdonald Physics Building at McGill and about continuing work at Manchester. He and Soddy had suspected that alpha particles might be helium atoms, but they hadn't been able to prove it. He pointed out that any stable element resulting from a radioactive transformation should be found in the radioactive minerals. "This lends support to the suggestion already put forwards, that possibly helium is an ultimate product of the disintegration of one of the radioactive elements, since it is only found in radioactive minerals."

He touched on the difficulty of proving this: "While the whole train of evidence we have considered indicates with little room for doubt that the α-particle is a projected helium atom, there was still wanting a decisive and incontrovertible proof of the relationship."

Then he described an experiment that he and Hans Geiger had performed in Manchester. They requested the glassblower, Baumbach, manufacture a double-walled tube with the thinnest possible glass on the inside. Radium emanation was placed in the inside tube. The thin walls would allow alpha particles to pass through, but hold the emanation particles back. The space outside the inner tube was under a vacuum. "After some days a bright spectrum of helium was observed

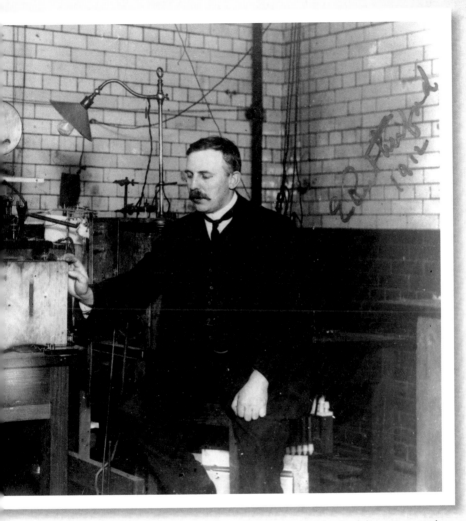

Ernest Rutherford (right) and Hans Geiger in the physics laboratory at the University of Manchester, England, in 1912

in the outer vessel." To counter the objection that the helium came from the tube with the emanation, the tube was emptied and helium was added. After several days, no helium was found in the outer tube. "We may thus confidently conclude that the α-particles themselves give rise to helium, and are atoms of helium."

The Latin inscription on his Nobel medal, translated, said, "It is a good thing to have brought life to perfection by skills/knowledge that have been discovered." Rutherford was a young Nobel winner, only thirty-seven years old.

Rutherford had first investigated and named alpha rays. Now he had deciphered what they really are. When they are shot out of a radioactive atom, the particle is a helium ion, missing two electrons. It quickly grabs electrons from neighboring gases, giving rise to the ionizing effects seen from radioactivity.

One of the benefits of winning the Nobel was a cash award of about 7,000 pounds, almost five years of Rutherford's usual salary. He sent cash presents to his parents and his brothers and sisters, generously sharing his fortune. He also sent a note of thanks and cash to Jacob Reynolds, his former teacher from Havelock. He wrote, "You will have seen some time ago that I was awarded a Nobel Prize, and am sure you will be pleased at the success of your old student.... In these later days I have not properly thanked you for the way you initiated me into the mysteries of Latin, Algebra and Euclid [geometry] in my youthful days.... The start I got with you stood me in good stead when I went to Nelson." He also bought a car, and he enjoyed stuffing it full of students and taking off for an afternoon of touring.

Researchers who worked with Rutherford knew firsthand that he had a temper. At the same time, he was often friendly and would sit for several minutes inquiring about research progress.

His students were guided by his experience but also allowed considerable leeway in what they investigated. Most of the researchers referred to him as "Papa." One claimed that "even the laziest worker was bound to be infected with something of his interest and enthusiasm, or at worst to be imbued with a healthy desire to avert his active disapproval.... Newcomers soon learnt that the sight of Rutherford singing lustily 'Onward, Christian Soldiers'... as he walked round the corridors was an indication that all was going well."

One of Rutherford's Manchester colleagues was Dr. Hans Geiger. Together they determined to find a way to count the alpha particles emitted from radioactive substances. The way it had been done was uncomfortable and unreliable. A person would sit in a tea crate in a completely dark room for twenty to thirty minutes to allow their eyes to become accustomed to the dark and dilate as full as possible. Then the experiment would start. Alpha particles make tiny sparkles of light, called scintillations, when they hit a phosphorescent zinc sulfide screen. The experimenter peered through a microscope to magnify the scintillations and counted them as they appeared. The work was tedious. Rutherford lacked the patience to sit there, but he praised Geiger, saying "Geiger is a demon at the work and could count at intervals for a whole night without destroying his equanimity. I damned vigorously after two minutes and retired from the conflict."

Rutherford and Geiger devised a better way to count alpha particles that used the ionizing capacity of the particle. Two glass tubes were connected with an extremely tiny hole, only large enough for one alpha particle to pass at a time. The first tube collected the alpha particles that then passed through the hole into the second tube, where

An early Geiger counter

they ionized the gas and caused an electrical current that could be measured. Hans Geiger later invented the well-known radioactivity meter known as the Geiger counter. His design was based on the work he did with Rutherford.

Part of Geiger's responsibilities at the University was teaching new students about measuring radioactivity. In 1909, he informed Rutherford that an undergraduate student, Ernest Marsden, was ready for a research project.

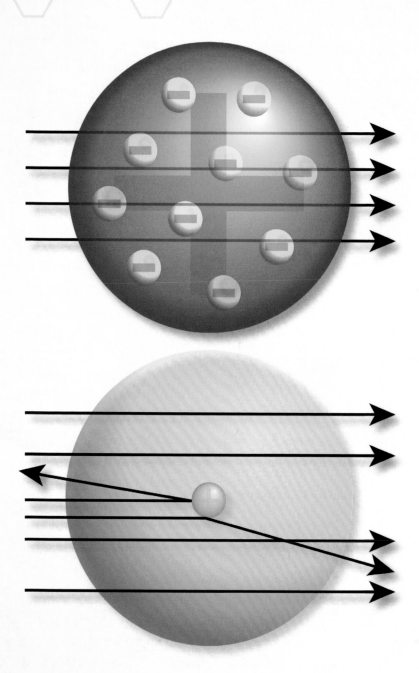

Atomic Models

The view of the structure of the atom in 1909 had come from a collaboration between J. J. Thomson and Lord Kelvin. After Thomson had discovered the electron, he and Kelvin had hypothesized what was called the "plum pudding" model of the atom: a shapeless glob of positive charge with the negatively charged electrons studded through it like plums in a pudding. Marsden's experiments would lead Rutherford to propose a more accurate structure of the atom.

Ernest Marsden was the son of a Lancashire, England, cotton weaver and came to the University of Manchester as an undergraduate. Rutherford initially assigned him the project of counting the deflected alpha particles. As is recounted in one of the many Rutherford stories, when Geiger asked about a project for Marsden, Rutherford said, "Why not let him see if any alpha-particles can be scattered through a large angle?"

The equipment for the scattering experiments consisted of a lead box shielding an alpha particle source with a slit to release them, a vacuum chamber into which the alpha particles were fired, sheets

Illustration of Rutherford's
gold foil experiment results

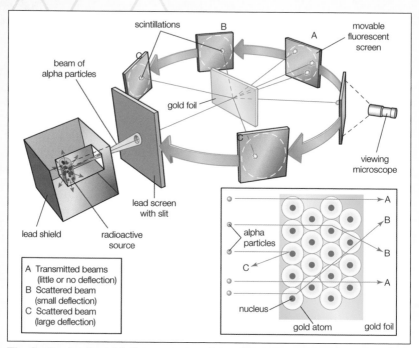

scintillations

B

A

movable
fluorescent
screen

beam of
alpha particles

gold foil

viewing
microscope

lead screen
with slit

lead shield

radioactive
source

alpha
particles

C

nucleus

gold atom

gold foil

A

B

B

A

A Transmitted beams
   (little or no deflection)
B Scattered beam
   (small deflection)
C Scattered beam
   (large deflection)

The Rutherford gold-foil experiment showed atoms not to be a uniform substance, rather, their mass is concentrated in a nucleus.

of metal, and a phosphorescent zinc sulfide screen target. The hits of alpha particles produced scintillations on the screen that were viewed and counted through a microscope attached to the chamber.

Alpha particles are released in all directions from a radioactive sample. With the sample enclosed in the lead box, only those near the slit would come out. If the alpha particles traveled in a straight line, the scintillations should line up in the same shape as the slit in the lead box from which they emerged. Rutherford had noticed years before while experimenting in Canada that passing a beam of alpha particles through a thin mica sheet led to a fuzzy line on the target. He had filed that information away, but now that Marsden was going to investigate this phenomenon, Rutherford intended to use alpha particles to probe inside the atom.

Marsden and Geiger set up the equipment and began firing alpha particles through different types of metal foil. They found that metals with heavier atomic weights deflected the alpha particles more than those with lighter weights. For example, gold with an atomic weight of 197 scattered the particles twice as much as silver (atomic weight 108) and twenty times more than aluminum (atomic weight 27).

Obviously, something in the thin metal foils was deflecting the alpha particles. To the great surprise of the researchers, they found that a tiny amount of the alpha particles were bounced back toward the source at angles greater than 90°. Rutherford later said, "It was as though you had fired a fifteen-inch shell at a piece of tissue paper and it had bounced back and hit you."

Marsden and Geiger published a paper in June 1909 on the scattering experiments, and then both men moved on to other projects. Marsden eventually left England and became a physics professor back in Rutherford's home country of New Zealand.

Meanwhile, Rutherford continued to contemplate the results of Geiger and Marsden's experiments. In December 1910, he wrote to a scientist friend at Yale University, "I think I can devise an atom much superior to Thomson's for the explanation of and stoppage of alpha-and-beta particles, and at the same time I think it will fit in extraordinarily well with the experimental numbers."

In the lab, Rutherford said, as Geiger remembered, "[T]hat he now knew what the atom looked like and how to explain the large deflections of the alpha particles."

In January 1911, Rutherford wrote his colleague and later his biographer, A. S. Eve, "Among other things I have been interesting myself in devising a new atom to explain some of the scattering results. It looks promising and we are now comparing the theory with experiments." Rutherford often performed experiments, considered the results until he had a hypothesis to fit, and then carried out more experiments to prove the theory.

Rutherford's view of the atom was not the amorphous mass that J. J. Thomson had proposed. Rutherford envisioned an atom of mostly empty space. Electrons circled on the outside edges of the atom and in the center was a tightly packed charged mass. In a paper entitled, "The Scattering of the Alpha and Beta Rays and the Structure of the Atom," Rutherford wrote:

> It is well known that the alpha and beta particles are deflected from their rectilinear path by encounters with the atoms of matter...There seems to be no doubt that these swiftly moving particles actually pass through the atomic system, and the deflexions observed should throw light on the electrical structure of the atom.... It seems that these large deviations of the α particle are produced by a single atomic encounter....A simple calculation shows that the atom must be the seat of an intense electric field in order to produce such a large deflexion at a single encounter. Considering the evidence as a whole, it seems simplest to suppose that the atom contains a central charge distributed through a very small volume.

At this early time, Rutherford was not sure whether the central mass was positively or negatively charged. His calculations showed that the center was one-trillionth of an inch in size, but held 3,999/4,000 of the mass. The electrons were the rest of the mass. He compared his model to the solar system, with electrons orbiting the center. The electrical force of the center repelled alpha particles causing the deflection of the path and the bouncing back at great angles.

There was a huge problem with Rutherford's model. As the electrons circle the center of the atom, they should lose energy and eventually fall into the center, causing the atom to collapse. Even with the power of centrifugal force from the circling orbit, the electron would lose energy. However, as we know, most atoms are stable, so something besides centrifugal force must be holding the electrons in their place. Another famous scientist would come up with the solution.

The Earth's solar system

Niels Bohr was a Danish postdoctoral researcher at the Cavendish Laboratory. He heard Rutherford speak at the annual dinner at the Cavendish and was intrigued by the big, happy New Zealand scientist. He was not happy at the Cavendish, so he wrote asking Rutherford if he could transfer to Manchester. Rutherford asked him to clear the transfer with J. J. Thomson because he didn't want to take students away from him. Thomson agreed and another spectacular team formed.

Soon Bohr and Rutherford together introduced the model of the atom that we understand today.

The first laboratory research that Rutherford assigned Bohr did not interest Bohr, but he soon told Rutherford that he had an idea to stabilize the Rutherford atom model. Bohr was a theoretical physicist, working on paper or blackboard and using equations rather than experiments.

In his model, Bohr used the quantum theories proposed by Max Planck, a German physicist. In working with electromagnetic radiation, which had been described as a wave, Planck had introduced the startling hypothesis that electromagnetic radiation not only behaved as a wave, but also contained tiny packets of energy he called quanta. Planck then developed a mathematical constant, h, which calculates the size of the quantum.

Niels Bohr

Bohr's theory was that electrons circle the center of the atom only in certain paths, called energy levels. An electron would not give off energy as long as it remained in one level. It changed levels by gaining or losing energy. When Bohr looked at the amount of energy required to jump from one level to another, he found that it could only be calculated using h, Planck's constant.

At first, Bohr's theory was only applied to the hydrogen atom. Though it seemed right on paper, there had been no experimental evidence for energy levels of electrons. After his time at the University of Manchester, Bohr returned to Denmark and continued working on the problem. He found that the energy levels shown by the spectrum of hydrogen matched his predictions for the quanta released in his theory and wrote a paper on his work with the hydrogen atom.

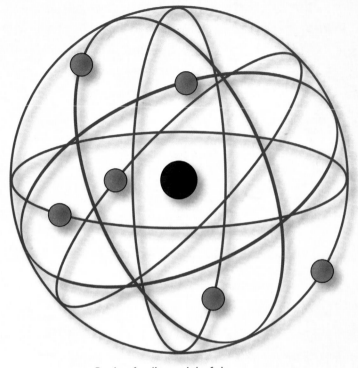

Rutherford's model of the atom

Rutherford received Bohr's paper and was thrilled with the additional proof for his model of the atom. However, he wrote back, "There appears to me one grave difficulty in your hypothesis, which I have no doubt you fully realize, namely, how does an electron decide what frequency it is going to vibrate at when it passes from one stationary state to the other? It seems to me that you would have to assume that the electron knows beforehand where it is going to stop."

Other scientists would take up the task of figuring out this part of the model. Years later, in 1923, Rutherford said, "A radical departure from accepted views seemed essential if progress were to be made.... But the test of any theory is its power to suggest new relations, and in this respect Bohr's theory was triumphant from the first."

The Rutherford-Bohr atom model is almost identical to what we understand today. There have been some modifications in the theory of atomic orbitals, but basically we see the atom as having a central mass with circling electrons that remain in energy levels until energy is applied or taken away.

According to one scientist, "Rutherford's nuclear theory of the atom... changed the whole face of modern physics."

Another student came along to reinforce Rutherford's model and to make discoveries of his own. Henry Moseley came from an established scientific family in England. Moseley discovered that the frequencies of x-rays probing crystals of elements increased in a periodic manner. He designated this whole number, Z, and it went up one unit from one element to the next in the Periodic Table. The explanation could be found in Rutherford's model; Z is the charge on the nucleus of the atom. "There is a fundamental quality in the atom which increases by regular steps as we pass from one element to the next," Moseley established. "This quality can only be the charge on the central positive nucleus." This discovery led to the adoption of the atomic number, which is calculated by the number of positively charged protons in the atom, as the organizing factor of the Periodic Table, rather than the atomic weights.

At the end of 1913, Moseley left Manchester and returned to Oxford to continue his research. He wrote a letter of gratitude to Rutherford: "I want you to know how very much I have enjoyed the three years spent in your department . . . Especially I want to thank you and Mrs. Rutherford for your kindness in interesting yourselves about me, and for the debt I owe you for personally teaching me how research work ought to be done." Rutherford had high hopes for more scientific breakthroughs from Moseley, but it was not to happen.

In 1914, new honors came to Rutherford. He was knighted by King George V, giving him the title Sir Ernest Rutherford. He wrote to his friend and biographer, A. S. Eve, "it was very unexpected and

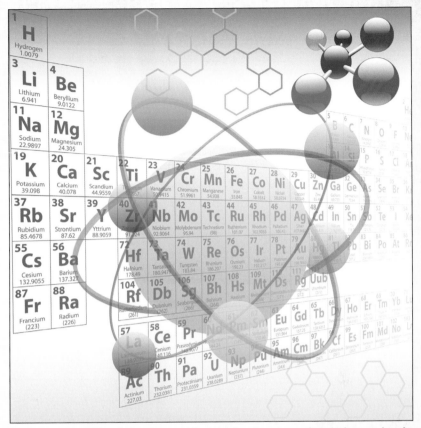

The periodic table of elements with models of an atom (center), a molecule (top right), and a chemical formula (top center)

not altogether desirable, for I feel such forms of recognition are not very suitable to people like myself. However, I am, of course, pleased at this public recognition of my labours, and hope that my activity will not be lessened by this transformation." He told another friend about his twelve-year-old daughter's reaction: "Eileen was very pleased with the news, and was greatly excited on New Year's Day with the succession of telegrams. She is of the opinion that neither of her parents has the 'swank' and natural dignity for such decorations." Rutherford had to buy court attire; black silk tail coat, white silk waistcoat, knee breeches, black silk stockings, cocked hat and sword. Eileen said he looked like a very superior footman.

8

Honors and War Work

BY THE END of 1914, England was involved in what is now called World War I. Ernest and May Rutherford traveled to Australia in the summer of 1914. Ernest and Harry Moseley were both at an Australian Royal Society meeting when the word came of war. The Rutherfords continued their scheduled trip, returning to New Zealand, and then on to North America, where Rutherford visited former colleagues at McGill University in Canada and his many friends at universities in the United States.

Henry, or Harry as he was called by friends, Moseley returned home to England when war broke out. He was commissioned as a lieutenant in the Royal Engineers and rose to the rank of captain. He landed with British troops on the Gallipoli Peninsula of Turkey on August 6, 1915. Four days later, the Turks attacked at dawn and Moseley was killed. Rutherford wrote an obituary and a plea for the government to realize how valuable scientists could be behind the lines. It was published in *Nature*:

British troops landing in Gallipoli
during World War I in 1915

Scientific men of this country have viewed with min-
gled feelings of pride and apprehension the enlistment
in the new armies of so many of our most promising
young men of science—with pride for their ready and
ungrudging response to their country's call, and with
apprehension of irreparable losses to science...Mose-
ley's fame securely rests on his fine series of investigations, and his remarkable record of four brief years'
investigation led those who knew him best to prophesy
for him a brilliant scientific career....It is a national
tragedy that our military organization at the start
was so inelastic as to be unable, with a few exceptions,
to utilize the offers of services of our scientific men
except as combatants in the firing line. Our regret
for the untimely death of Moseley is all the more poi-
gnant because we recognize that his services would
have been far more useful to his country in one of the
numerous fields of scientific inquiry rendered necessary by the war than by the exposure to the chances
of a Turkish bullet.

Other students and colleagues of Rutherford's were also caught
up in the war. E. N. Andrade, a student and later a biographer of
Rutherford, was in the British artillery. James Chadwick, soon to be a
colleague, was working on a fellowship in Berlin when the war broke
out. He was put in a prison camp for the duration of the war. Even
though the living space for Chadwick and five other men was a smelly
horse stall at a former horse racing course, he managed to set up a
laboratory to continue experiments. Hans Geiger was able to scrounge
some equipment for Chadwick. For a radioactive source, Chadwick
used a German toothpaste that contained thorium, which was added
to several beauty products as a guarantee of whiter teeth and softer
skin. The health risks were not fully understood at the time.

Fifty years later, Andrade remembered the effect of the war on the lab at Manchester: "The coming of the war in August 1914 naturally broke up completely the family life, for such it was, of the laboratory. The majority of laboratory workers were dispersed and Rutherford's attention was diverted to problems of national importance."

This photograph of a drawing, made for the *New York Herald* and the *London Sphere*, shows the R. M. S. *Lusitania* as a second torpedo hits behind a gaping hole in the hull.

Many of Rutherford's former researchers were on the other side of the war. Hans Geiger was drafted as a German artillery officer and was wounded. Otto Hahn helped develop and test poisonous gas that was used for the first time at Ypres in April 1915. Years later, during World War II, Hahn would refuse to work on the atomic bomb for Germany.

In Denmark, Niels Bohr was neutral, and sometimes forwarded to Rutherford letters from Germany.

The Great War, as it was called then, lasted from August 1914 to November 1918. When it began, forces from England, France, and Russia, known as the Allies, were on one side with the Central Powers, including Germany and Austria-Hungary on the other. In 1917, the United States joined on the side of the Allies. Eventually, casualties mounted up to nearly 10 million troops killed and another 21 million wounded.

On May 7, 1915, a German submarine torpedoed and sunk the British ship *Lusitania*. The British government realized that there was a need for a defense against submarines. Rutherford was one of the scientists asked to work on the project.

Rutherford thought the best way to detect submarines underwater would be to track the sounds they made. He began a series of tests to develop underwater microphones that could distinguish submarine sounds from other noises. Unfortunately, the British Royal Navy was not very supportive. Rutherford's teams were given a small boat to sail about on Scotland's Firth of Forth. Part of Rutherford's job was holding on to the legs of Sir Richard Paget while his head was underwater trying to identify sounds. Rutherford wrote to his mother, "I spent three days hard at work on a converted 'trawler' and I expect to go up again shortly....We heard last night of the submarining of a troop ship in the Aegean with a loss of 1,000 lives."

Rutherford's experimental approach to science carried over to his war work. He wrote, "We have found in testing diaphragms it is very important to avoid grease on them and make certain that bubbles of air are not attached to the diaphragm."

Rutherford and other scientists completed research on both passive methods of hearing submarines, such as microphones in the water, and active systems that send out sound waves that would bounce off the submarines. This more active method of detecting submarines and other objects under the water came to be known as sonar.

After the United States entered the war in 1917, Rutherford went to America to demonstrate to American scientists his work on sub-

Thomas Edison in 1920

marine detection. He found that they had also been working on a similar project, although they were behind the British at the time. One famous American who was on the project was Thomas Edison, then eighty-years-old. Rutherford said, "I was received very well by the old man, who was as enthusiastic as a schoolboy over his ideas."

On Rutherford's return trip to England, he was on a ship with a unit of U. S. Marines. The Marines had a goat as a mascot. One night, Rutherford rang the steward because he found the goat under his bed. The steward told him, "It's quite all right, Sir, he's slept there every night so far!"

Rutherford could claim to be the inventor of sonar, but he found that another former colleague was also working on the idea. Paul Langevin, former friend from Cavendish Laboratory days, was working on sonar for the French. After the war, Rutherford heard that Langevin was claiming to be the inventor of sonar and Rutherford said, "If Langevin says he did it first, that's good enough...let Langevin have credit."

Early in the war, Ernest Marsden had been conducting experiments under Rutherford's supervision. He bombarded hydrogen gas with alpha particles and observed that some of the hydrogen atoms were flying further than expected. His conclusion was that they were coming from the radioactive material used. Marsden wrote two papers on the research and then left England to become head of the physics department at the University of New Zealand, with Rutherford's recommendation. Then he left that university to serve for a time in New Zealand Expeditionary Force during the war.

It was only after Marsden had left Manchester that Rutherford had a chance to read his papers. Marsden's conclusion seemed wrong to Rutherford, so he wrote asking Marsden if he would mind if he conducted some experiments on the same idea. Marsden replied that he did not mind.

The equipment used by Rutherford for what turned out to be a groundbreaking series of experiments can still be seen at the Cavendish Laboratory. It consists of a small brass tube, two glass valves and brass extensions and joints sealed by the red sealing wax that Rutherford always used.

In the midst of his experiments, Rutherford missed an Anti-Submarine Division meeting, sending the message, "If, as I have reason to believe, I have disintegrated the nucleus of the atom, this is of greater significance than the war." In December 1917, he wrote to Niels Bohr, "I have got, I think, results that will ultimately have great importance. I am detecting and counting the light atoms set in motion by alpha particles and the results, I think, throw a great deal of light on the character and distribution of forces near the nucleus." He continued, "I am also trying to break up the atom by this method. . . . Regard this as private."

After hundreds of experiments with different gases, Rutherford found that when nitrogen was bombarded with alpha particles, hydrogen nuclei were released. He concluded that the alpha particles were chipping away parts of the nitrogen atoms—the hydrogen nucleus that was released—and the nitrogen atoms became oxygen atoms because of the loss of the particles. This was induced transmutation—changing one stable element into another—in contrast to the transmutation that takes place naturally with radioactive elements.

Marsden had conducted the first atom-splitting experiments, but it took Rutherford to decipher what was happening.

The hydrogen nuclei, labeled by Marsden as the H-particle, that was expelled from the nitrogen atom was a single positively-charged particle which Rutherford called the proton. Because it was a lighter weight than the alpha particle, the proton traveled further and hit the phosphorescent screen with a brighter scintillation.

When Marsden came home from war, he stopped in Manchester to tell Rutherford that he would return to the University of New Zealand. Rutherford immediately said, "You'll stay with us, of course. I want to show you something." He showed Marsden the experiments he had completed. He had sealed one end of the brass cylinder with silver foil to prevent passage of alpha particles while allowing the protons to pass through. He demonstrated his equipment to Marsden first by using air and then oxygen, carbon dioxide, and water vapor. Each time no scintillations occurred. Then he placed nitrogen gas in the cylinder and scintillations lit up the screen.

Rutherford's hypothesis was that alpha particles (helium ions) were striking the nitrogen atoms and chipping away a hydrogen ion and leaving an oxygen atom. So, helium + nitrogen = hydrogen + oxygen. Rutherford realized that these experiments could eventually provide the capability to visualize the interiors of more elements. However, first more powerful particles would be required. "If alpha particles—or similar projectiles—of greater energy were available for future experiments, we might expect to break down the nucleus structure of many of the lighter atoms."

Niels Bohr saw the value of Rutherford's experiments. He said this accomplishment "in the course of time was to give rise to such tremendous consequences as regards man's mastery of the forces of nature."

In the meantime, Rutherford was in the process of changing jobs. His former mentor, J. J. Thomson, had decided to retire from the director position at the Cavendish Laboratory. His recommendation was that Rutherford be appointed in his place.

9

Back to Cavendish

RUTHERFORD WAS RETURNING to his scientific roots—the Cavendish Laboratory. He wrote his mother about the decision: "It was a difficult question to decide whether to leave Manchester as they have been very good to me, but I felt it probably best for me to come here, for after all it is the chief physics chair in the country and has turned out most of the physics professors of the last twenty years. It will of course be a wrench, pulling up my roots again and starting afresh to make new friends, but fortunately I know a few good people here already and will not be a stranger in Trinity College."

Students at the University of Manchester presented Rutherford with a gold stopwatch as he prepared to leave the school.

One of the difficulties Rutherford faced at Cavendish was the huge influx of men returning from war. They intended to take up their interrupted university careers and space had to be found for them. Some proposed that more space might be available if women were not allowed to enter the university. Rutherford objected vigorously to this idea. On December 6, 1920, he and the chemistry professor wrote a letter to the *Times:*

Rutherford (right) in Cavendish Laboratory
with Irish physicist Ernest Walton

For our part, we welcome the presence of women in our laboratories on the ground that residence in this University is intended to fit the rising generation to take its proper place in the outside world, where, to an ever increasing extent, men and women are being called upon to work harmoniously side by side in every department of human affairs. For better or for worse, women are often endowed with such a degree of intelligence as enables them to contribute substantially to progress in the various branches of learning; at the present stage in the world's affairs we can afford less than ever before to neglect the training and cultivation of all the young intelligence available. For this reason, no less than for those of elementary justice and of expediency, we consider that women should be admitted to degrees and to representation in our University.

This was not a change in Rutherford's views. While he was at McGill, he had encouraged and worked with a young woman, Harriet Brooks, and he had admired the work of Marie Curie and her daughter, Irène Joliot-Curie, for years.

The struggle to find the money to provide space for the deluge of students and to refurbish the rundown lab was difficult for Rutherford. He hated to beg for money, except for radioactive supplies for his researchers, and he did not want to be responsible to any donors. He preached frugality and innovation to his students. This mentality also was shown by the lab steward, Frederik Lincoln. As the story goes, when a student came to Lincoln asking for a length of one-inch pipe for an experiment, Lincoln handed him a hacksaw and pointed to an old bicycle leaning up against the wall. "Just cut off some of the handlebar," he said.

The problem with Rutherford's usual benchtop experiments and conservative view of expenses was that the advances in physics meant that future experiments would require more sophisticated equipment. The experiments of the next generation would be accomplished with the help of multimillion-dollar instruments.

Rutherford continued to be boisterous and loud as he aged. In a famous photograph, Rutherford is shown under a sign installed at the Cavendish, saying "Talk Softly Please." Researchers complained that his booming voice caused vibrations that upset delicate instruments. Once, when he was preparing to make a radio broadcast from Cambridge, England, to Cambridge, Massachusetts, one of his men said, "Why use radio?"

In 1920, Rutherford was invited to give his second Bakerian Lecture to the Royal Society. In 1904, he had spoken about radioactivity, including the particles released in the process. In the 1920

Rutherford giving a BBC radio broadcast in the early 1930s

Lecture, he speculated about the existence of a "heavy hydrogen" that had a nucleus of two units rather than one. He also mentioned the possibility of a lighter helium atom with three units of mass rather than four; and he wondered about another particle that might be found in the atomic nucleus. "It seems very likely... [that there is] an atom of mass 1 which has zero nuclear charge." Heavy hydrogen was indeed discovered later, as was light helium.

Rutherford's proposal about a neutral particle led a physicist named James Chadwick to investigate. Chadwick eventually discovered what is called the neutron—a particle with no charge that is part of the atomic nucleus. Chadwick stated, "I just kept pegging away. I did quite a number of silly experiments.... I must say the silliest were done by Rutherford." Those silly experiments led Chadwick to his discovery. He also remembered, "Before the experiments we had to accustom ourselves to the dark, to get our eyes adjusted…we sat in this dark room, dark box, for perhaps half an hour or so, and naturally talked.…It was those conversations that convinced me the neutron must exist."

It took ten years for the discovery to be made. Chadwick read of work by Marie Curie's daughter, Irène, and her husband, Frédéric Joliot-Curie. They had bombarded the element beryllium with alpha particles and observed a strange radiation from it. They had not read of Rutherford's prediction of a neutral particle embedded in the atomic nucleus. So they missed the discovery of the neutron. Chadwick, however, replicated their experiment and found that the particle released had the mass of a proton but had no electrical charge. For this work, Chadwick was awarded the 1935 Nobel Prize for physics. That same year, the Joliot-Curies won the award for chemistry.

The presence of the neutron partially explained why positively charged protons can pack into the nucleus without the forces of repulsion blasting the atom apart. The neutral particles help reduce the forces.

In 1921, an interesting young man arrived at the Cavendish from Russia. Peter Kapitza came on a mission to buy equipment to send back to Russia but decided to stay in England. He had trained as an electrical engineer. As a new student at the Cavendish, Kapitza was assigned to the usual course taught by Chadwick in a small room called "The Nursery." In this elementary course, usually lasting about six months, beginning researchers were schooled in lab techniques and radioactivity theory. Kapitza finished the course in two weeks.

Kapitza went on to conduct some experiments with alpha particles in a cloud chamber, which had been invented by another Cavendish researcher. Alpha particles leave visible tracks in the moist atmosphere of the chamber. Kapitza studied the effects of strong magnetic fields on alpha particles. Soon, however, his influence persuaded Rutherford that bigger, more powerful machines were needed.

It was time to move away from the brass cylinders, glass tubes, and sealing wax Rutherford had used.

Kapitza wrote to his mother about Rutherford, "Generally speaking, however, he is a fierce character. When he is displeased—look out. He will not mince words, no sir. But what an amazing noodle! He has a distinctly unique mind. His instinct and intuition are colossal. I could never imagine anything like it before I have been attending his lectures and talks. He expresses himself very clearly. He is an absolutely exceptional physicist and a most original human being."

Kapitza's nickname for Rutherford was "Crocodile." In later years, Anna Kapitza, Peter's second wife, said, "In Russia the crocodile is the symbol for the father of the family and is also regarded with awe and admiration because it has a stiff neck and cannot turn back. It just goes straight forward with gaping jaws—like science, like Rutherford." The truth of the origin of the nickname is not known, since time could have made Anna's explanation more fanciful than true. However, when a new laboratory was built in the courtyard of the Cavendish to house Kapitza's research, he convinced a sculptor to engrave a drawing of a crocodile near the front entrance.

The new laboratory, the Royal Society Mond Laboratory, opened in 1933, and Kapitza was named the director. He continued his experiments into the effects of magnetism on the atom under Rutherford's supervision.

Russia had been taken over by communists in 1917 and renamed the Soviet Union. Kapitza traveled back and forth from England to the Soviet Union frequently. Then in 1934, the Soviet government prevented his return to the Cavendish. Kapitza's wife, still in England, came to Rutherford and told him that the Soviets were holding Kapitza and insisted that he work for their government. Rutherford pulled all the diplomatic strings he could to have Kapitza returned, but he failed. The Soviet ambassador in London wrote Rutherford, "Cambridge would no doubt like to have all the world's greatest scientists in its laboratories, in much the same way the Soviet Union would like to have Lord Rutherford and others of your great physicists in her laboratories."

When Rutherford realized that Kapitza would not be allowed to return, he arranged to have a duplicate of the Mond Laboratory, including the etching of the crocodile, shipped to Kapitza, brick by brick and including all the equipment. The Soviet Union paid 30,000 pounds for the equipment and shipping. But Rutherford knew that the equipment was already obsolete.

Kapitza was in a deep depression over not returning, but eventually he pulled himself together and went back to work. He won the 1978 Nobel Prize in Physics, partly based on work done under Rutherford.

In 1925, Rutherford made a trip home to New Zealand, where he was feted and welcomed. He told one group of listeners, "I have always been very proud of the fact that I am a New Zealander." He gave a public lecture where he tried to demonstrate the size of the atom. "If 100,000,000 people counted at the rate of 100 a minute it would take about 1,000 years for them to count the atoms in gas occupying a space the size of the end of my thumb.... If a pea in the middle of the Hall might represent the nucleus...then the electrons would be as far away as the walls."

A funny slip of the tongue happened at Rutherford's old college town of Nelson. The mayor said, "Ladies and gentlemen today this little boy from our district has risen to be head of the biggest lavatory in the world where the mysteries of nature are found out."

Rutherford realized that to understand any more about the atomic nucleus, more energetic bombarding particles were needed. He had estimated that only one or two alpha particles in a million transformed a nitrogen atom in his experiments. In a speech as the president of the Royal Society in November 1927, Rutherford wished for "atoms and electrons which have an individual energy far transcending that of the alpha and beta-particles from radioactive bodies. I am hopeful that I may yet have my wish fulfilled, but it is obvious that many difficulties will have to be surmounted before this can be realized." Actually, the men who would accomplish the feat had just arrived at Cavendish.

T. E. Allibone had previously worked at the electrical company, Metropolitan-Vickers, commonly known as Metrovick. He was working on a way to accelerate electrons using massive amounts of steady, electrical power. John Cockcroft had also worked at Metrovick, and came to Cambridge to work on a doctorate in math. They were joined by Irishman Ernest Walton who arrived at Cavendish courtesy of an Exhibition of 1851 Scholarship—the same one that had brought Rutherford to Cambridge more than thirty years before.

The expectation was that it would take five to eight million volts to accelerate particles to speeds that would penetrate the atomic nucleus. Other scientists in the United States and in Germany, besides those at the Cavendish in England, were seeking a method to accelerate particles. The race for the best method to split the atom was on.

Rutherford (center) in May 1932 with Ernest Walton (left) and John Cockcroft

Allibone and Cockcroft worked on building transformers that would produce a steady current. After working a few years, Allibone returned to Metrovick, but Cockcroft continued his research. He read a paper by Russian scientist George Gamow that demonstrated that alpha particles were capable of "tunneling" their way out of a nucleus rather than blasting their way out with high power. Cockcroft hypothesized that accelerated protons could also tunnel their way out at a much lower power setting than had previously been thought. Cockcroft and Walton began building the equipment needed to conduct their experiment.

After the equipment was built, Cockcroft and Walton tinkered with their setup, checking for leaks and testing components. Rutherford suspected that they were procrastinating, delaying the actual operation of the equipment, and was worried that one of the other research groups would get first results. He encouraged them to hurry.

On April 14, 1932, Walton first tried the setup. He remembered: "When the voltage and the current of protons reached a reasonably high value, I decided to have a look for scintillations. . . . Immediately I saw scintillations on the screen. I then went back to the control table and switched off the power to the proton source. On returning to the hut no scintillations could be seen. After a few more repetitions of this kind of thing, I became convinced that the effect was genuine."

Walton phoned Cockcroft who came quickly and also viewed the scintillations. He called Rutherford who came immediately. Walton recalled: "With some difficulty we maneuvered him [Rutherford] into the rather small hut and he had a look at the scintillations. He shouted out instructions such as 'switch off the proton current,' 'increase the accelerator voltage,' etc. but he said little or nothing about what he saw. He ultimately came out of the hut, sat down a stool and said something like this: 'Those scintillations look mighty like alpha-particle ones. I should know an alpha-particle scintillation when I see one for I was in at the birth of the alpha-particle and I've been observing them ever since.'"

Rutherford's boys had split the atom. They had won the race! By bombarding a lithium target with protons, they released alpha particles, meaning the protons had split the lithium atoms. Lithium has an atomic weight of seven; add one for the proton and you get a total of eight. When the split occurs, two alpha particles—atomic weight four—are released. For their work, they received the Nobel Prize in physics for 1951.

Ernest Rutherford and his daughter, Eileen, outside a cottage in Wales in 1928

Other momentous events happened to Rutherford in 1930—both sad and happy occasions. His daughter, Eileen, had married a mathematician, Ralph Fowler. Rutherford often talked of scientific ideas with Fowler. He relied on Fowler's theoretical background to strengthen his understanding.

May traveled to New Zealand for a visit even though she worried about Eileen, who was pregnant with her fourth child. She felt she needed to visit her elderly mother. She and Rutherford wrote letters to keep up with family news from both sides of the world. On December 14, Rutherford telegraphed, "Eileen baby daughter and us all well." Two days after the birth, Eileen along with most of the household caught a severe gastrointestinal virus. Everyone seemed to be on the road to recovery so, on December 23, Rutherford planned to attend a dinner at Trinity College. But Eileen's nurse arrived with the news that she had died from a blood clot. Rutherford telegraphed May, "Eileen died suddenly but peacefully Wed. evening. Embolism. Baby well." Eileen was only twenty-nine. The four grandchildren continued to be a bright part of Rutherford's life.

Two weeks after Eileen's death, Rutherford learned that he was being ennobled, or designated Lord Rutherford. As he wrote May, "This means a Peerage and membership in the House of Lords.... Of course I do not intend to make any difference in our mode of life.... I ought to recognize that it is in a sense a personal tribute to my work as well as to the importance of science to the state." He telegraphed his mother, "Now Lord Rutherford. More your honour than mine." He chose his title "Lord Rutherford of Nelson" in honor of "my birthplace and home of my grandfather."

10

The Loss of Crocodile

R ESEARCHERS WHO WORKED with Rutherford were always amazed by his knowledge and enthusiasm about their experiments. One student, Australian Mark Oliphant, remembered finishing a long experiment at the end of the day. He and his colleague decided they would develop the photographic records of the experiment the next day. However, Rutherford had different ideas. "I can't understand," he thundered. "Here you have exciting results and you are too damned lazy to look at them tonight." Another time, Oliphant's phone rang at 3 in the morning. It was Rutherford and he said, "'Oliphant. I'm sorry to disturb you at this time of the morning but I think I know what those little particles are."

"What are they Sir?"

"They're helium particles of mass 3."

"How could you possibly say that? What reasons can you have for conclusion?" "Reasons! Reasons! Oliphant, I feel it in my water." It turned out that Rutherford was right.

In 1936, Rutherford turned sixty-five but showed no sign of slowing down. A journalist wrote of him, "He wears his years very

A 1934 painting of Ernest
Rutherford by Oswald Birley

lightly and vigorously. He has no time to worry about such little things as growing old. He is too much absorbed with the present."

When he wasn't in the lab, Rutherford spent time with Eileen's children. Another favorite leisure time activity was golf. Rutherford played on a foursome and it was a rowdy, loud group. When a golfer would drop out, Rutherford was known to say, "Ah! He couldn't stand the rough and tumble of a Trinity foursome."

From left to right: Rabbi Nehemiah Mossessohn, Albert Einstein, Chaim Weizmann, and Zionist leader Menahem Ussishkin

For his whole life, Rutherford had enjoyed reading. He was particularly fond of detective stories and biographies. The librarians at the Cavendish often had difficulties keeping up with his insistent demands for new books to read.

Although Rutherford had never been politically active, other than trying to get Peter Kapitza's release from the Soviet Union, affairs sometimes led him to intervene on the part of other scientists. In 1933, Adolf Hitler came to power in Germany. Jewish scientists and others who held beliefs Hitler considered undesirable lost their jobs and were persecuted. Rutherford's friend Chaim Weizmann, head of Hebrew

University in Jerusalem, asked English scientists to raise funds to help Jewish scientists and teachers to get out of Germany. Other scientists were also asking for help from English scientists. The Academic Assistance Council was formed to handle these requests and Rutherford became its president. One member recalled Rutherford's reaction, "As we talked, he exploded with wrath at Hitler's treatment of scientific colleagues whom he knew intimately and valued."

Rutherford's political activity was not viewed favorably by everyone. He received hate mail but carried on. The Royal Society was convinced to provide office space for the group. At one large fundraising meeting Albert Einstein was the main speaker. He had fled Germany and was now living in the United States. Rutherford's efforts allowed 507 refugees to find permanent positions and another 308 to get temporary jobs.

In 1937, Rutherford was still healthy and seemed to be always on the go. But his health wasn't perfect. He had a small hernia that occasionally bothered him, and he wore a truss to support it and keep it from hurting. A hernia is a small rip in the abdominal muscle. Sometimes, as with Rutherford, a part of the bowel can poke through the hernia. If the abdominal muscles contract, the part of the bowel is pinched off and a strangulated hernia results. The only cure for it is immediate surgery.

On Thursday, October 12, 1937, Rutherford was doing chores in his wife's garden. He fell from a low branch of a tree he was trimming. The next day he was vomiting and in pain, and May took him to a man who sometimes did massages for people. He had helped relieve the pain when Rutherford had hurt a knee. But the man saw that Rutherford needed professional attention, so the family doctor was called.

The doctor diagnosed the condition as strangulated hernia, and Rutherford was taken to a facility for surgery. The operation was performed and Rutherford seemed to be recovering. May telegraphed his family in New Zealand: "Ernest operated on for strangulated hernia operation successful doing nicely."

However, his bowels did not start working properly again. Doctors realized that nothing else could be done. He grew steadily weaker and died on October 19. His last words to May were, "I want to leave 100 pounds to Nelson College. You can see to it. Remember a hundred to Nelson." At the end of his life he remembered the small New Zealand college where he got his academic start.

The news of Rutherford's death reached his colleagues in Bologna, Italy, who were there to celebrate the bicentennial of the birth of Luigi Galvani, inventor of batteries. When the telegram arrived, Niels Bohr approached the platform with tears streaming down his face and informed the audience of Rutherford's death. He also spoke of "the debt which science owed so great a man whom he was privileged to call both his master and his friend."

In the Soviet Union, Kapitza mourned the loss of Crocodile, as he had called Rutherford, and he wrote to Bohr, "I loved Rutherford…I learned a great deal from Rutherford—not physics but how to do physics." The *New York Times* eulogized him with "He was universally acknowledged as the leading explorer of the vast, infinitely complex universe within the atom, a universe that he was the first to penetrate."

Rutherford's ashes were buried at Westminster Abbey, near other famous scientists such as Isaac Newton, Michael Faraday, and Lord Kelvin.

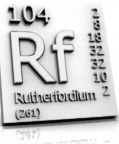

Rutherford received many honors in his memory, but the most appropriate honor is seen on the Periodic Table, where element number 104 is named rutherfordium or rf.

Timeline

1871   Born in New Zealand on August 30

1890   Wins scholarship to attend Canterbury
           College, University of New Zealand

1892   Awarded BA degree

1893   Awarded MA degree

1894   Finishes BS degree

1895   Wins an Exhibition of 1851 scholarship and goes to Cavendish
           Laboratory at Cambridge University, England

1898   Characterizes and names alpha and beta particles; chosen
           professor at McGill University, Montreal, Canada

1900   Marries May Newton

1901   Daughter, Eileen, is born

1903   Publishes, along with Soddy, theory of radioactive
           decay; becomes member of Royal Society

1904   Publishes *Radio-activity* and proposes use of half-life
           to determine age of the earth

1907   Becomes physics department chair at the
           University of Manchester

1908   Awarded the Nobel Prize in chemistry

1911   Discovers structure of atom from bombardment experiments

1913   Publishes *Radioactive Substances and their Radiations*

1914   Knighted

1915   Works on anti-submarine techniques

1917   Transmutes nitrogen into oxygen by
           bombardment with alpha particles

1919   Returns to Cavendish Laboratory

1920   Calls the hydrogen nucleus the proton
           and theorizes about the neutron

1925   Becomes president of Royal Society

1930   Daughter dies

1931   Becomes Lord Rutherford of Nelson

1933   Becomes president of Academic Assistance
           Council to help German scientists

1937   Dies on October 19

Sources

Chapter One: New Zealand Boy

p. 11,   "all knowledge . . . " Richard Reeves, *A Force of Nature: The Frontier Genius of Ernest Rutherford* (New York: Atlas Books, 2008), 24.

p. 11,   "This book has been written . . . " Ibid., 26-27.

p. 12,   "At one time . . ." Ibid., 25.

p. 13,   "Mr. Rutherford . . . ." John Campbell, *Rutherford: Scientist Supreme*, Christchurch (New Zealand: AAS Publications, 1999), 18.

pp. 14–15,   "If they are mustered . . ." Reeves, *A Force of Nature: The Frontier Genius of Ernest Rutherford*, 25.

p. 15,   "the boat capsized . . ." Campbell, *Rutherford: Scientist Supreme*, 36

pp. 15–16,   "Mr. and Mrs. Rutherford . . ." Ibid.

p. 16,   "He had such powers . . ." David Wilson, *Rutherford: Simple Genius*, (Cambridge, MA: MIT Press, 1983), 34.

p. 17,   "He was a fine teacher . . ." Ibid., 36.

p. 17,   "the science teaching . . ." Ibid.

Chapter Two: Off to Other Parts

p. 20,   "The college hall . . ." Campbell, *Rutherford: Scientist Supreme*, 98.

p. 23,   "I learnt more of research . . ." Ibid., 119.

p. 23,   "miserable, cold, draughty . . ." Naomi Pasachoff, *Ernest Rutherford: Father of Nuclear Science* (Berkeley Heights, NJ: Enslow Publishers, Inc., 2005), 34.

p. 24,   "iron still keeps . . ." Campbell, *Rutherford: Scientist Supreme*, 166.

p. 25,   "He was entirely hopeless . . ." Reeves, *A Force of Nature: The Frontier Genius of Ernest Rutherford*, 29.

p. 26,   "From the first . . ." Wilson, *Rutherford: Simple Genius*, 45.

p. 26,   "Personally Mr. Rutherford . . ." A. S. Eve, *Rutherford: Being the Life and Letters of the Rt. Hon. Lord Rutherford, O. M.* (New York: The MacMillan Company, 1939), 12.

p. 26,   "Of course Rutherford's papers . . ." Campbell, *Rutherford: Scientist Supreme*, 171.

p. 26,   "The Science Scholarship awarded . . ." Ibid., 187.

p. 27,   "The fact is that . . ." Ibid., 188.

p. 27,   "Maclaurin declines . . ." Ibid.

p. 27,   "That's the last potato . . ." Ibid., 192.

p. 27,   "I am afraid you will have . . ." Ibid., 209.

p. 27,   "The result of being in love . . ." Ibid.

Chapter Three: New Rays and New Research

p. 29,   "I shall be very glad . . . " Eve, *Rutherford: Being the Life and Letters of the Rt. Hon. Lord Rutherford, O.M.*, 14.

p. 29,   "The country is pretty enough . . ." Ibid., 15.

pp. 29–30,   "I went to the Lab . . . " Ibid.

p. 30,   "where I saw his wife. . ." Ibid.

p. 30,   "best little kid I have . . ." Ibid.

p. 32,   "We ordinary Cambridge . . ." Wilson, *Rutherford: Simple Genius*, 69.

p. 32,   "many of them . . ." Campbell, *Rutherford: Scientist Supreme*, 215.

pp. 32–33,   "We've got a rabbit . . . " Ibid., 225.

p. 33,   "You can't imagine . . ." Ibid., 236.

p. 33,   "Rutherford began his work . . ." Pasachoff, *Ernest Rutherford: Father of Nuclear Science,* 45.

p. 33,   "The reason I am so keen . . ." Ibid., 46.

p. 35,   "The discovery . . ." Ibid., 48.

p. 35,   "I am a little full up . . ." Ibid., 49.

p. 35,   "The professor of course . . ." Ibid., 48.

p. 36,   "I can see no escape . . ." "3 Experiments, 1 Big Idea," Web site of the American Institute of Physics.

p. 36,   "jolly little beggars . . ." Wilson, *Rutherford: Simple Genius,* 114.

p. 39,   "Rutherford . . . investigated the radiation . . ." Pasachoff, *Ernest Rutherford: Father of Nuclear Science,* 50-51.

p. 39,   "is quite in the first . . ." Ibid., 51.

Chapter Four: McGill and Montreal

p. 41,   "I have never had . . ." Campbell, *Rutherford: Scientist Supreme,* 248.

pp. 41–42, "As far as I can . . ." Reeves, *A Force of Nature: The Frontier Genius of Ernest Rutherford,* 43.

p. 42,   "my chances . . ." Pasachoff, *Ernest Rutherford: Father of Nuclear Science,* 54.

p. 42,   "to start work . . ." Eve, *Rutherford: Being the Life and Letters of the Rt. Hon. Lord Rutherford, O.M.,* 53.

p. 42,   "Rejoice with me . . ." Ibid., 55.

p. 43,   "I am expected . . ." Campbell, *Rutherford: Scientist Supreme,* 247.

p. 44,   "It sounds rather . . ." Ibid.

p. 44,   "Calculus is fine . . ." Reeves, *A Force of Nature: The Frontier Genius of Ernest Rutherford,* 49.

p. 44,   "I am very pleased . . ." Eve, *Rutherford: Being the Life and Letters of the Rt. Hon. Lord Rutherford, O.M.,* 64.

p. 44,   "emanation," Pasachoff, *Ernest Rutherford: Father of Nuclear Science,* 57.

p. 45,   "My dear girl . . ." J. L. Heilbron, *Ernest Rutherford and the Explosion of Atoms* (Oxford: Oxford University Press, 2003), 36.

p. 45,   "In addition to . . ." Wilson, *Rutherford: Simple Genius,* 137.

p. 46,   "Mother is writing . . ." Campbell, *Rutherford: Scientist Supreme,* 259.

p. 46,   "You have probably . . ." Eve, *Rutherford: Being the Life and Letters of the Rt. Hon. Lord Rutherford, O.M.,* 76.

p. 47,   "The existence of bodies . . ." Wilson, *Rutherford: Simple Genius,* 148.

p. 47,   "Chemical evidence . . ." Ibid.

p. 47,   "Recent advances . . ." Ibid., 148-149.

pp. 47–48, "Possibly Professor . . ." Ibid., 150.

p. 49,   "(1) That there is a constant . . ." Ibid., 224.

Chapter Five: Transmutation?

p. 51,   "Rutherford, this is transmutation . . ." Reeves, *A Force of Nature: The Frontier Genius of Ernest Rutherford,* 51.

p. 52,   "that the development . . .of Faraday," Wilson, *Rutherford: Simple Genius,* 155.

p. 52,   "we had stumbled . . ." Ibid.

p. 52,   "I have to keep . . ." Pasachoff, *Ernest Rutherford: Father of Nuclear Science,* 58.

p. 53,   "To put it bluntly . . ." Wilson, *Rutherford: Simple Genius,* 157.

p. 53,   "By the time . . ." Pasachoff, *Ernest Rutherford: Father of Nuclear Science,* 58-59.

p. 54,   "A tribute of my respect . . ." Ernest Rutherford, *Radio-activity* (Cambridge Physical Series: Cambridge, England, 1905), dedication page.

p. 54,   "The close of the old . . ." Ibid., 1.

p. 54,   "the cause of the disruption . . ." Ibid., 248.

p. 54,   "There is thus reason . . ." Ernest Rutherford, *Radio-activity*, 247.

p. 54,   "there is no reason . . ." Reeves, *A Force of Nature: The Frontier Genius of Ernest Rutherford*, 56.

p. 55,   "Could a proper . . ." Ibid.

p. 55,   "Some fool in a laboratory . . ." Ibid.

p. 56,   "to the author . . ." Pasachoff, *Ernest Rutherford: Father of Nuclear Science*, 63.

p. 56,   "diffusing science . . ." Ibid., 64.

p. 57,   "there was an *internal* . . ." Eve, *Rutherford: Being the Life and Letters of the Rt. Hon. Lord Rutherford, O.M.,* 107.

p. 57,   "I came into the room . . ." Ibid.

p. 57,   "Rutherford was so . . ." Pasachoff, *Ernest Rutherford: Father of Nuclear Science*, 68.

p. 58,   "My old friend . . ." Reeves, *A Force of Nature: The Frontier Genius of Ernest Rutherford*, 58.

p. 58,   "a splendid subject . . ." Wilson, *Rutherford: Simple Genius,* 255.

p. 58,   "adopting Mr. Rutherford's manner . . ." Barbara Goldsmith, *Obsessive Genius: The Inner World of Marie Curie* (New York: Atlas Books, 2005), 105.

p. 59,   "I go to Philadelphia . . ." Eve, *Rutherford: Being the Life and Letters of the Rt. Hon. Lord Rutherford, O.M.,* 147.

p. 59,   "It is certainly . . ." Ibid.

p. 59,   "I am staying . . ." Ibid., 148.

Chapter Six: Winning the Nobel

p. 61,   "I have not mentioned . . ." Reeves, *A Force of Nature: The Frontier Genius of Ernest Rutherford*, 61.

p. 61,   "The fine laboratory . . ." Pasachoff, *Ernest Rutherford: Father of Nuclear Science*, 70.

p. 62,   "the determining factor . . . " Ibid., 71.

p. 62,   "By thunder!" Reeves, *A Force of Nature: The Frontier Genius of Ernest Rutherford*, 63.

p. 62,   "Youthful, energetic . . ." Ibid., 65.

p. 63,   "I have retained . . ." Wilson, *Rutherford: Simple Genius,* 226.

p. 63,   "If I am to have . . ." Pasachoff, *Ernest Rutherford: Father of Nuclear Science*, 72.

p. 63,   "for his investigations . . ." Official Web site of the Nobel Prize Foundation, the Nobel Prize in Chemistry 1908, www.nobelprize.org.

p. 63,   "I must confess . . ." Eve, *Rutherford: Being the Life and Letters of the Rt. Hon. Lord Rutherford, O.M.,* 183.

p. 63,   "all science . . . " Reeves, *A Force of Nature: The Frontier Genius of Ernest Rutherford*, 70.

p. 64,   "*A ALPHA RAY . . .*" Campbell, *Rutherford: Scientist Supreme,* 313.

p. 65,   "Rutherford's discoveries . . ." K. B. Hasselberg, "The Nobel Prize in Chemistry 1908" (Award Ceremony Speech, December 10, 1908), http://nobelprize.org.

p. 65,   "Though Rutherford's work . . ." Ibid.

p. 65,   "Everyone says he . . ." Campbell, *Rutherford: Scientist Supreme,* 317.

p. 66,   "This lends support . . ." Ernest Rutherford, Nobel Lecture, December 10, 1908, http://nobelprize.org.

p. 66,   "While the whole train . . ." Ibid.
pp. 66–67, "After some days . . ." Ibid.
p. 67,   "We may thus . . ." Ibid.
pp. 67–68, "It is a good thing . . ." Campbell, *Rutherford: Scientist Supreme,* 316.
p. 68,   "You will have seen . . ." Ibid., 319.
p. 68,   "even the laziest worker . . ." Pasachoff, *Ernest Rutherford: Father of Nuclear Science,* 75-76.
p. 69,   "Geiger is a demon . . ." Reeves, *A Force of Nature: The Frontier Genius of Ernest Rutherford,* 77.

Chapter Seven: Atomic Models

p. 71,   "Why not let him see . . ." Wilson, *Rutherford: Simple Genius,* 291.
p. 73,   "It was as though . . ." Ibid.
p. 73,   "I think I can devise . . ." Ibid., 295.
p. 73,   "[T]hat he now knew . . . " Reeves, *A Force of Nature: The Frontier Genius of Ernest Rutherford,* 80.
p. 73,   "Among other things I have . . ." Campbell, *Rutherford: Scientist Supreme,* 337.
p. 74,   "It is well known . . ." Reeves, *A Force of Nature: The Frontier Genius of Ernest Rutherford,* 81.
p. 77,   "There appears to me one grave . . ." Eve, *Rutherford: Being the Life and Letters of the Rt. Hon. Lord Rutherford, O.M.,* 221.
p. 77,   "A radical departure . . ." Pasachoff, *Ernest Rutherford: Father of Nuclear Science,* 84.
p. 78,   "Rutherford's nuclear theory . . ." Ibid., 85.
p. 78,   "There is a fundamental quality . . ." Reeves, *A Force of Nature: The Frontier Genius of Ernest Rutherford,* 90.
p. 78,   "I want you to know . . ." Eve, *Rutherford: Being the Life and Letters of the Rt. Hon. Lord Rutherford, O.M.,* 235.
pp. 78–79, "it was very unexpected . . ." Campbell, *Rutherford: Scientist Supreme,* 347.
p. 79,   "Eileen was very pleased . . ." Ibid., 348.

Chapter Eight: Honors and War Work

p. 82,   "Scientific men . . ." Eve, *Rutherford: Being the Life and Letters of the Rt. Hon. Lord Rutherford, O.M.,* 247-248.
p. 83,   "The coming of the war . . ." Pasachoff, *Ernest Rutherford: Father of Nuclear Science,* 87.
p. 84,   "I spent three days hard . . ." Reeves, *A Force of Nature: The Frontier Genius of Ernest Rutherford,* 100.
p. 84,   "We have found . . ." Ibid.
p. 85,   "I was received . . . " Ibid., 101-102.
p. 85,   "It's quite all right . . ." Eve, *Rutherford: Being the Life and Letters of the Rt. Hon. Lord Rutherford, O.M.,* 262.
p. 85,   "If Langevin says . . ." Pasachoff, *Ernest Rutherford: Father of Nuclear Science,* 89.
p. 86,   "If, as I have reason . . ." Reeves, *A Force of Nature: The Frontier Genius of Ernest Rutherford,* 95.
p. 86,   "I have got . . ." Ibid., 102.
p. 86,   "I am also trying . . ." Campbell, *Rutherford: Scientist Supreme,* 376.
p. 87,   "You'll stay with us . . ." Reeves, *A Force of Nature: The Frontier Genius of Ernest Rutherford,* 97.

p. 87,   "If alpha particles . . ." Ibid., 104.
p. 87,   "in the course of time . . ." Pasachoff, *Ernest Rutherford: Father of Nuclear Science,* 89-90.

Chapter Nine: Back to Cavendish

p. 89,   "It was a difficult question . . ." Wilson, *Rutherford: Simple Genius,* 413.
p. 90,   "For our part . . ." Reeves, *A Force of Nature: The Frontier Genius of Ernest Rutherford,* 109-110.
p. 90,   "'Just cut off some of . . ." Ibid., 113.
p. 91,   "Why use radio?" Ibid.
p. 91,   "It seems very likely . . ." Pasachoff, *Ernest Rutherford: Father of Nuclear Science,* 94.
p. 91,   "I just kept . . ." Reeves, *A Force of Nature: The Frontier Genius of Ernest Rutherford,* 115.
p. 92,   "Before the experiments . . ." Ibid., 116.
p. 92,   "The Nursery," Ibid., 123.
p. 93,   "Generally speaking . . ." Campbell, *Rutherford: Scientist Supreme,* 388.
p. 93,   "In Russia the crocodile . . ." Ibid.
pp. 93–94, "Cambridge would . . ." Ibid., 128.
p. 94,   "I have always been . . ." Campbell, *Rutherford: Scientist Supreme,* 403.
p. 94,   "If 100,000,000 people . . ." Ibid.
p. 94,   "Ladies and gentlemen . . . " Ibid., 411.
pp. 94–95, "atoms and electrons . . . " Heilbron, *Ernest Rutherford and the Explosion of Atoms,* 111, 113.
p. 96,   "When the voltage . . . " Wilson, *Rutherford: Simple Genius,* 561.
p. 96,   "With some difficulty . . . " Ibid.
p. 97,   "Eileen baby daughter . . ." Campbell, *Rutherford: Scientist Supreme,* 422.
p. 97,   "Eileen died suddenly . . ." Ibid.
p. 97,   "This means a Peerage . . . " Ibid., 424.
p. 97,   "Now Lord Rutherford . . ." Ibid.
p. 97,   "my birthplace . . . " Ibid.

Chapter Ten: The Loss of Crocodile

p. 99,   "'I can't understand . . ." Campbell, *Rutherford: Scientist Supreme,* 463.
p. 99,   "'Oliphant. I'm sorry . . ." Ibid., 465.
pp. 99–100, "He wears his years . . ." Pasachoff, *Ernest Rutherford: Father of Nuclear Science,* 104.
p. 100,   "Ah! He couldn't . . ." Eve, *Rutherford: Being the Life and Letters of the Rt. Hon. Lord Rutherford, O.M.,* 410.
p. 101,   "As we talked . . ." Campbell, *Rutherford: Scientist Supreme,* 456.
p. 101,   "Ernest operated . . . " Eve, *Rutherford: Being the Life and Letters of the Rt. Hon. Lord Rutherford, O.M.,* 472.
p. 102,   "I want to leave . . ." Reeves, *A Force of Nature: The Frontier Genius of Ernest Rutherford,* 168.
p. 102,   "the debt which science . . ." Campbell, *Rutherford: Scientist Supreme,* 474.
p. 102,   "I loved Rutherford . . ." Ibid.
p. 102,   "He was universally . . ." Reeves, *A Force of Nature: The Frontier Genius of Ernest Rutherford,* 169.

Bibliography

Campbell, John. *Rutherford: Scientist Supreme.* AAS Publications, Christchurch, New Zealand, 1999.

Cathcart, Brian. *The Fly in the Cathedral.* Farrar, Straus and Giroux, New York, 2004.

Eve, A. S. *Rutherford: Being the Life and Letters of the Rt. Hon. Lord Rutherford, O. M.* The MacMillan Company, New York, 1939.

Goldsmith, Barbara. *Obsessive Genius: The Inner World of Marie Curie.* Atlas Books, New York, 2005.

Heilbron, J. L. *Ernest Rutherford and the Explosion of Atoms.* Oxford University Press, Oxford; 2003.

Pasachoff, Naomi. *Ernest Rutherford: Father of Nuclear Science.* Enslow Publishers, Inc., Berkeley Heights, NJ, 2005.

Reeves, Richard. *A Force of Nature: The Frontier Genius of Ernest Rutherford.* Atlas Books, New York, 2008.

Rutherford, Ernest. *Radio-activity.* 2nd ed. Cambridge Physical Series, Cambridge, England, 1905.

Sinclair, Keith, ed. *The Oxford Illustrated History of New Zealand.* Oxford University Press, Oxford, 1990.

Wilson, David. *Rutherford: Simple Genius.* The MIT Press, Cambridge, MA, 1983.

Web Sites

Woodrow Wilson Leadership Program in Chemistry, The Chemical Heritage Foundation
http://www.chemheritage.org/classroom/chemach/atomic/rutherford.html

New Zealand chemistry
http://www.chemistry.co.nz/ernest_rutherford.htm

The New Zealand Edge
http://www.nzedge.com/heroes/rutherford.html

Eric Weisstein's World of Scientific Biography
http://scienceworld.wolfram.com/biography/Rutherford.html

Index

Picture Credits